1097
m
Br

THE NEW SOUTH
AND OTHER ADDRESSES

BY

HENRY WOODFIN GRADY

With Biography, Critical Opinions, and Explanatory
Notes

BY

EDNA HENRY LEE TURPIN

HASKELL HOUSE PUBLISHERS LTD.
Publisher of Scarce Scholarly Books
NEW YORK. N. Y. 10012
1969

First Published **1904**

HASKELL HOUSE PUBLISHERS Ltd.

Publishers of Scarce Scholarly Books

280 LAFAYETTE STREET

NEW YORK. N. Y. 10012

Library of Congress Catalog Card Number: **68-24979**

Standard Book Number 8383-0948-8

Printed in the United States of America

Henry Grady: His Life and Work

When Mr. Grady was introduced to a Boston audience he accounted for himself humorously by saying, " My father was an Irishman and my mother was a woman. I come naturally by eloquence." The brilliant young Southerner, quick of wit and of temper, warm-hearted, enthusiastic, fervid of imagination, was a fine type of the Irish-American. His father, William Grady, by energy and integrity accumulated an independent fortune. He moved from North Carolina to Georgia, and soon after married Miss Gartrell, a woman of much sweetness and strength of character.

Their son, Henry Woodfin Grady, was born May 24, 1851, in Athens, Georgia. As a boy he evinced the sympathetic nature which inspired him when a man. " Dear mother," he would call from his bed on winter nights, " do you think the servants have enough cover? It is so cold and I want them to be warm." He had generous thoughts and kind words for every little ragamuffin that he met. From school or street he often sent home such notes as this: " Dear mother, please give this child something to eat. He looks so hungry. H. W. G." Such a note was always a passport to the hospitality of his home. It was a grief to him to see any one angry or unhappy, and more than one poor or delicate child was protected by his ready wit and strong arm. At school he excelled more in athletic sports and outdoor games than in studies, but he was an omnivorous reader.

Upon Henry Grady's happy childhood fell the shadow which darkened the Southern homes of the early sixties. At the first call to arms, William Grady volunteered in the Confederate army. He organized and equipped at his own expense a cavalry company of which he was elected captain and went to Virginia, the battle ground of the Confederacy. He bore himself with such valor that he was promoted on the field, but while his friends were glorying in his gallantry he fell in battle before Petersburg. His grief-stricken widow was left to rear their children, a daughter and two sons. This duty she fulfilled with loving wisdom.

Henry Grady was graduated from the University of Georgia in 1868. He was never a close student and gave to his text-books only the time necessary to enable him to rise from class to class. But he read widely, especially history and fiction, and every character of Dickens was as familiar to him as were the comrades of his classroom. After his graduation from Athens, he went to the University of Virginia, where his oratorical powers distinguished him in literary and debating societies.

Soon after his return to Georgia he wrote some clever newspaper letters, the success of which led him to adopt journalism as a career. These letters were signed " King Hans," a fanciful union of his own name with that of Miss Julia King, the first

sweetheart of his boyhood, who became the wife of
his young manhood. Her charms of person and
character blessed his home, and his own happiness
made him more eager for the happiness of others.
Lovable everywhere, he always turned his best side
to his own hearthstone, to his beloved wife and son
and daughter.

Pursuing his journalistic work, Mr. Grady moved
to Rome and took charge of the *Courier*. One day
a "ring," political or financial, was discovered in
Rome and he wrote a vehement editorial in de-
nunciation of it. The proprietor of the paper ob-
jected to its publication, fearing that it would of-
fend some of his patrons. Young Mr. Grady had
strong views and some money of his own. That
very day he bought Rome's two other newspapers,
the *Daily* and the *Commercial,* and his attack on
the "ring"— which was crushed — appeared in the
Daily-Commercial next morning. He ran his paper
with erratic ability. One week news-columns and
editorials would sparkle with his wit and wisdom,
the next week it would be left to the foreman's
editorship.

When his paper failed — and failure was inevi-
table under such management — Mr. Grady went
to Atlanta, and, with two other gentlemen brilliant
and enterprising like himself, founded the *Atlanta-
Herald.* They determined to edit the best newspaper in the South, and pursued their course with
reckless disregard of financial considerations. The
Herald's most formidable rival was the *Constitution.*
Both papers wished to reach middle Georgia to
which there was no morning train from Atlanta. In

the heat of competition each ran a special engine a hundred miles to carry a thousand papers. The *Herald* and the *Constitution* went to press about the same time, and every morning there was an exciting race to the station. The one which got there first was given the main line and on this the day's sales largely depended. These special trains absorbed the entire earnings of both papers, and brought them to the verge of failure. A mortgage on the *Herald* was foreclosed and the *Constitution* survived, financially crippled. Mr. Grady had not only lost the money left from his Rome venture but was involved in debt. He tried to establish a weekly paper but the effort was unsuccessful. His plans, novel in conception and execution, were not adapted to a small city and a meager purse.

Borrowing fifty dollars from a friend, he gave twenty dollars to his wife and bought a ticket to New York City to get as far as possible from the scene of his failure. With only three dollars in his pocket, without friends and influence, he reached the metropolis. Here is the story of his experience as told by himself:

"After forcing down my unrelished breakfast on the morning of my arrival in New York, I went out on the sidewalk in front of the Astor House, and gave a bootblack twenty-five cents, one-fifth of which was to pay for shining my shoes and the balance was a fee for the privilege of talking to him. I felt that I would die if I did not talk to somebody. Having stimulated myself at that doubtful fountain of sympathy, I went across to the *Herald* office, and the managing editor was good enough to admit me to his sanctum. It happened that just at that time several of the Southern States were holding constitutional conventions. The *Herald* manager asked me if I knew anything about politics. I replied that I knew very little about anything else. 'Well,' said he, 'sit at this desk and write me an article on state conventions in the South.' With these words he tossed me a pad and left me alone in the room. When my task-master returned, I had finished the article and was leaning back in the chair with my feet up on the desk. 'Why, Mr. Grady, what is the matter?' asked the managing editor. 'Nothing,' I replied, 'except that I am through.' 'Very well; leave your copy on the desk, and if it amounts to anything I will let you hear from me. Where are you stopping?' 'I am at the Astor House.'

"Early the next morning before getting out of bed, I rang for a hallboy and ordered the *Herald*. I actually had not strength to get up and dress myself, until I could see whether or not my article had been used. I opened the *Herald* with a trembling hand, and when I saw that 'State Conventions in the South' was on the editorial page, I fell back on the bed, buried my face in the pillow, and cried like a child. When I went back to the *Herald* office that day the managing editor received me cordially and said, 'You can go back to Georgia, Mr. Grady, and consider yourself in the employ of the *Herald*.'"

Mr. Grady's articles on Southern topics in the *New York Herald* and the *Atlanta Constitution* gained

wide reputation, especially in Georgia and throughout the South.

In 1880, through the financial aid of friends, he
bought a fourth interest in the *Constitution* and
gave up all outside work to devote his time and attention to the duties of managing editor. At last
he had found his work. He threw himself into it
heart and soul, inspired by success and the consciousness of power. Like Horace Greeley, he was
" a journalist because he had something to say
which he believed mankind would be the better for
knowing, not because he wanted something for himself which journalism might secure for him."

Busy with news and politics, he yet found time
for whatever would develop home resources and
industries, and turn the streams of investment into
Southern channels. His articles were a mixture of
shrewd common sense and fervid fancy, of convincing statistics and irresistible prose poems.

No one man ever did more to upbuild and develop
a section than did Mr. Grady to the South, desolated
by war and ravaged by reconstruction misrule. His
busy hand and brain were behind the success of the
Atlanta fairs of 1880, 1886, and 1888. The Young
Men's Christian Association building and the Confederate Soldiers' Home were beneficiaries of his pen
and his purse. He suggested and fostered the public
improvements, the educational institutions, and the
industrial enterprises of Atlanta. As if they had
been his own, he worked to develop the marble
quarries and the coal fields of Georgia, and the iron
fields of Alabama.

No class appealed more to his sympathy than the

impoverished Southern farmers, facing new conditions and labor problems. His suggestions to
them were always practicable and often unique.
He urged diversified farming. He advised the planting of watermelons for Northern shipment, and it
was his keen and hopeful eye which first saw the
fortune in Florida oranges.

Mr. Grady himself had an intense love for rural
scenes and avocations, and it was his dream to own
a suburban farm. In his busy life this dream never
became a reality, but he loved to describe its spring
in the grove of oak trees, its meadows of orchard
grass and clover, its herd of mild-eyed Jerseys, its
colts frolicking in the barley patch. Many a time,
weary with the incessant demands on his time and
patience, he would shut his office door with a bang
and instruct the boy to tell all callers that " he had
gone to his farm." There his busy mind rested and
reveled.

Great as was Mr. Grady's interest in industrial
development, it was even greater in intellectual
culture and moral issues. Says Walter B. Hill:
" He whose pen seemed like the touch of Midas,
turning to the gold of material wealth every interest to which it pointed, taught also that impera-
tive lesson of our needy time — that to know and to
be are greater things than to get and to have." He
organized the Piedmont Chautauqua, which was an
intellectual but not a financial success. With his
usual unselfishness, he insisted on bearing the lecture
expenses and protecting from loss the capitalists —
quite willing to be protected — who went in on his
account. The generous and public-spirited man

mortgaged his own home to save this educational institution.

Indeed, amid all the successful enterprises which he fostered, Mr. Grady remained comparatively poor. His business faculty — and it was unusual — was given to the public. A great newspaper, a beautiful young city, factories, marble quarries, coal and iron mines, farms more fertile and more profitable, a new prosperity throughout the South, bear witness to his ability. He was, as is well said, more than an optimist, he was the embodiment of that faith in the future which brings success and happiness. And he had a marvelous power of inspiring others with his enthusiasms — witness the instance of his city editor, who, reading Mr. Grady's glowing account of the profits in Irish potatoes, straightway planted a large crop.

Mr. Grady's sympathy went out especially to the young. He knew all the little army of boys employed in the *Constitution* office, and interested himself in the condition and character and ambition of each one. He was in his element when a circus came to town, and it was a familiar sight to see him heading a procession of children going to see the animals and enjoy the antics of the clown.

Wherever there was sorrow and suffering he was prompt with help and comfort. His intimate friend, Mr. Joel Chandler Harris, tells this charming story of him:

"He had a theory that the rich who have become poor by accident or misfortune, suffer the stings of poverty more keenly than the poor who have always been poor, for the reason that they are not qualified to fight against conditions that are at once strange and crushing. Several Christmases ago, I had the pleasure of witnessing a little episode in which he illustrated his theory to his own satisfaction as well as to mine.

"On that particular Christmas Eve, there was living in Atlanta an old gentleman who had at one time been one of the leading citizens of the town. He had in fact been a powerful influence in the politics of the state, but the war swept away his possessions and along with them all the conditions and surroundings that had enabled him to maintain himself comfortably. His misfortunes came on him when he was too old to begin the struggle with life anew with any reasonable hope of success. He gave way to a disposition that had been only convivial in his better days when he had hope and pride to sustain him, and he sank lower until he had nearly reached the gutter.

"I joined Mr. Grady as he left the office, and we walked slowly down the street enjoying the kaleidoscopic view of the ever-shifting, ever-hurrying crowd as it swept along the pavements. In all that restless and hastening throng there seemed to be but one man bent on no message of enjoyment or pleasure, and he was old and seedy-looking. He was gazing about him in an absent-minded way. The weather was not cold, but a disagreeable drizzle was falling.

"'Yonder is the Judge,' said Mr. Grady, pointing to the seedy-looking old man. 'Let's go and see what he is going to have for Christmas.'

"'I found out long afterwards that the old man

had long been a pensioner on Mr. Grady's bounty, but there was nothing to suggest this in the way in which the young editor approached the Judge. His manner was the very perfection of cordiality and consideration, though there was just a touch of gentle humor in his bright eyes.

" ' It isn't too early to wish you a merry Christmas, I hope,' said Mr. Grady, shaking hands with the old man.

" ' No, no,' replied the Judge, straightening himself up with dignity; ' not at all. The same to you, my boy.'

" ' Well,' remarked Mr. Grady lightly, ' you ought to be fixing up for it. I'm not as old as you are, and I've got lots of stirring around and shopping to do if I have any fun at home.'

" The eyes of the Judge sought the ground. ' No. I was- ah- just considering.' Then he looked up into the laughing but sympathetic eyes of the boyish young fellow, and his dignity sensibly relaxed. ' I was only- ah- Grady, let me see you a moment.'

"The two walked to the edge of the pavement, and talked together some little time. I did not overhear the conversation, but learned afterwards that the Judge told Mr. Grady that he had no provisions at home and no money to buy them with, and asked for a small loan.

" ' I'll do better than that,' said Mr. Grady. ' I'll go with you and buy them myself.— Come with us,' he remarked to me with a quizzical smile. ' The Judge here has found a family in distress, and we are going to send them something substantial for Christmas.'

" We went to a grocery store near at hand, and I saw, as we entered, that the Judge had not only recovered his native dignity, but had added a little to suit the occasion. I observed that his bearing was even haughty. Mr. Grady had observed it, too, and the humor of the situation so delighted him that he could hardly control the laughter in his voice.

" ' Now, Judge,' said Mr. Grady, as we approached the counter, ' we must be discreet as well as liberal. We must get what you think this suffering family most needs. You call off the articles, the clerk here will check them off, and I will have them sent to the house.'

" The Judge leaned against the counter with a careless dignity quite inimitable, and glanced at the well-filled shelves.

" ' Well,' said he, thrumming on a paper-box, and smacking his lips thoughtfully, ' we will put down first a bottle of chow-chow pickles.'

" ' Why, of course,' exclaimed Mr. Grady, his face radiant with mirth; ' it is the very thing. What next?'

" ' Let me see,' said the Judge, closing his eyes reflectively — ' two tumblers of strawberry jelly, three pounds of mincemeat, and two pounds of dates, if you have real good ones, and — yes — two cans of deviled ham.'

" Every article the Judge ordered was something he had been used to in his happier days. The whole episode was like a scene from one of Dickens' novels, and I have never seen Mr. Grady more delighted. He was delighted with the humor of it, and appreciated in his own quaint and charming way and to the fullest extent the pathos of it. He dwelt on it then and afterwards, and often said that he envied the broken-down old man the enjoyment of the luxuries of which he had so long been deprived.

"On a memorable Christmas day not many years after, Mr. Grady stirred Atlanta to its very depths by his eloquent pen, and brought the whole community to the heights of charity and unselfishness on which he always stood. He wrought the most unique manifestation of prompt and thoughtful benevolence that is to be found recorded in modern times. The day before Christmas was bitter cold, and the night fell still colder, giving promise of the coldest weather that had been felt in Georgia for many years. The thermometer fell to zero, and it was difficult for comfortably clad people to keep warm even by the fires that plenty had provided, and it was certain that there would be terrible suffering among the poor of the city. The situation was one that appealed in the strongest manner to Mr. Grady's sympathies. It appealed, no doubt, to the sympathies of all charitably-disposed people: but the shame of modern charity is its lack of activity. People are horrified when starving people are found near their doors, when a poor woman wanders about the streets until death comes to her relief; they seem to forget that it is the duty of charity to act as well as to give.

"Mr. Grady was a man of action. He did not wait for the organization of a relief committee, and the meeting of prominent citizens to devise ways and means for dispensing alms. He was his own committee. His plans were instantly formed and promptly carried out. The organization was complete the moment he determined that the poor of Atlanta should not suffer for lack of food, clothing, or fuel. He sent his reporters out into the highways and byways, and into every nook and corner of the city. He took one assignment for himself, and went about through the cold from house to house. He had a consultation with the Mayor at midnight, and cases of actual suffering were relieved then and there.

" The next morning, which was Sunday, the columns of the *Constitution* teemed with the results of the investigation which Mr. Grady and his reporters had made. A stirring appeal was made in the editorial columns for aid to the poor — such an appeal as only Mr. Grady could make. The plan of relief was carefully made out. The *Constitution* was prepared to take charge of whatever the charitably disposed might feel inclined to send to its office — and whatever was sent should be sent early.

" The effect of this appeal was astonishing — magical, in fact. It seemed impossible to believe that any human agency should bring about such a result. By eight o'clock on Christmas morning — the day being Sunday — the street in front of the *Constitution* office was jammed with wagons, drays, and vehicles of all kinds, and the office itself was transformed into a vast depot of supplies. The merchants and business men had opened their stores as well as their hearts, and the coal and wood dealers had given the keys of their establishments into the

gentle hands of charity. Men who were not in
business subscribed money, and this rose into a
considerable sum. When Mr. Grady arrived on the
scene, he gave a shout of delight, and cut up antics
as joyous as those of a schoolboy. Then he pro-
ceeded to business. He had everything in his head,
and he organized his relief trains and put them in
motion more rapidly than any general ever did. By
noon, there was not a man, woman, or child, white
or black, in the city of Atlanta that lacked any of
the necessaries of life, and to such an extent had
the hearts of the people been stirred that a large
reserve of stores was left over after everybody
had been supplied. It was the happiest Christmas
day the poor of Atlanta ever saw, and the happiest
person of all was Henry Grady."

Mr. Grady's interest in public questions was keen
and he was a political power throughout the South.
" He was almost an absolute dictator in Georgia
politics. No man cared to stand for election to any
place, high or low, unless he felt Grady was with
him. He was the most powerful factor in the election of two governors, and practically gave more
than one United States senator his seat." But after
the campaign was over, when others sought office,
he went back to his newspaper. Time after time
high positions were offered him and declined. Office
had no charm for him, but had he lived longer he
would almost inevitably have been drawn into public life by the people's need for the services of a
man so able and so honest.

In 1884, when the whole South was listening
eagerly for election returns, the busy wires brought

to the *Constitution* office news that Cleveland was elected. A brass band was procured and Mr. Grady and Captain Howell headed an enthusiastic procession to the capitol. Entering the hall of the House of Representatives, Mr. Grady said in impressive tones, " Mr. Speaker, a message from the American people."

" Let it be received," was the dignified response.

Mr. Grady seized the gavel from the Speaker's hand and cried, "In the name of God and the American people, I declare the House adjourned to celebrate . the election of Grover Cleveland, the first Democratic president in twenty-four years."

There were shouts of applause and the House broke up with the wildest enthusiasm. Mr. Grady often said that he and Oliver Cromwell were the only two men who ever adjourned a legislative body in that style.

But Mr. Grady's fame does not rest on his success as a journalist or his ability as a politician. His was the mission of peacemaker and interpreter between the North and the South. Appreciating the virtues on both sides, he realized that sectional animosity was largely the result of ignorance and misunderstanding and these he set himself to remove. His first opportunity to do this at the North was when he was invited to the banquet of the New England Society. His speech, breathing harmony, fraternity, and good-will, touched the keynote of the situation. He showed the people of both sections that we may love and honor the dead Confederacy with absolute loyalty and devotion to the restored Union.

This address on the "New South" was followed by a brilliant speech at Dallas, Texas, on the race problem. He was invited to deliver an address in Boston, and he prepared it with great and unusual care. All the powers of his intellect, his keen wit and gentle humor, his remarkable command of language, were devoted to this speech which reached the high water mark of elegant and florid oratory. It is Grady's best contribution to the higher politics of his country, and it was his last. He contracted a severe cold at the Boston banquet and was hardly able to give a short address the next evening before the Bay State Club. The friends who met him at the Atlanta station, prepared to give him enthusiastic reception, bore him home, ill with pneumonia. Instead of improving, his condition grew steadily worse. It was hard to realize that his brilliant and useful career had come to an end.

"He has work yet to do," said his physician.

"Perhaps his work is finished," said his mother, with truer insight.

His death on the 23d of December, 1889, cast a gloom over the Christmas festivities of Atlanta. Men spoke with trembling lips and women went about their daily task with tearful eyes.

Indeed, his death was a national calamity. Who could take his place as inspirer and prophet of Southern progress, as pacificator between the sections? He encouraged the development of home resources, put aside the animosities of war, and gave the North truer conceptions of the South. He was the embodiment of the new South of which he spoke, which, emulating with loving pride the virtues of the old, turns its face to the future and adapts itself to new conditions. What he said of another was pre-eminently true of him. " His leadership has never been abused, its opportunities never wasted, its powers never prostituted, its suggestions never misdirected."

Thanks are due from the editor of this book to the proprietors of the *Atlanta Constitution* and to the members of Mr. Grady's family for their courteous permission to use the speeches and biographical material in the Memorial Edition of Mr. Grady's works, and for their kindness in looking over the proof of this little volume.

Critical Opinions

'A citizen of Atlanta, he loved Georgia; a Georgian, he adored the South; a Southerner, he worshipped the whole Union. He was an American in the fullest sense of that term. There was no work of public or private charity among us which he did not aid by his tongue, his pen, his head, or his purse, whether that work was to procure the pardon of an abandoned young girl confined in the chain-gang with criminals, or canvassing the streets of Atlanta through snow and ice, accompanied with a retinue of wagons and drays, to accumulate fuel and provisions to prevent our poor from freezing and from starving. It was in response to his appeals, more than to all else combined, that a home is now being erected within sight of the dome of yonder capitol for the aged and infirm veterans of the Lost Cause. It was to him more than to all others that our Piedmont Expositions, designed to show to the world the wealth of our undeveloped mineral, agricultural, and other resources, were carried to a successful end. It was through his persuasive power that the Chautauqua Association, designed more thoroughly to educate our people, was established.

But in the limited time allotted to me, I cannot go into further details. If you seek his monuments, look around. They are in every home and every calling of life. In all that which has tended to develop the material resources of the country, to enrich his people, to encourage education and a love of the arts, to relieve suffering, to provide for the poor, and to make our people better and nobler, he devoted his life, unselfishly, and without hope of other reward than the approval of his conscience.— *Julius L. Brown*

Henry W. Grady was one of the youngest, the most brilliant, the best beloved of the young men of his country who, since the war of secession, won distinction in public life. Whether considered as a writer or an orator, his talents were extraordinary. His language was strong, refined, and, in its poetic warmth and elegance, singularly beautiful. But that which gave to it its greatest value and charm was the wisdom of the thought, the sincerity of the high conscience of which it was the expression. It was given to him as it is to so few — the ability to wed noble thoughts to noble words — to make the pen more convincing than the sword in argument, to make the tongue proclaim "the Veritas that lurks beneath the letter's unprolific sheath."

Henry W. Grady was, in the truest sense, an American; his love of country, his unselfish devotion to it, were unquestioned and unquestionable; but he sought to serve it best by best serving the South, which he so greatly loved and which so loved and honored him. It was the New South of human freedom, material progress — not the Old South of chattel slavery and material sluggishness — of which he was the representative, the prophet.

It was the South of to-day, which has put off the bitterness, defeats and animosities of the war; which has put on the sentient spirit of real union, of marvelous physical development, which advances day by day to wealth, dignity, and greatness by gigantic strides. This was the South that he glorified with pen and tongue, and which he sought with earnest, zealous love to bring into closer, warmer fraternity with the North and the North with it.—*Philadelphia Ledger*

The New South

On the 21st of December, 1886, Mr. Grady, in response to an urgent invitation, delivered the following Address at the Banquet of the New England
Club, New York:

" There was a South of slavery and secession
— that South is dead. There is a South of union
and freedom — that South, thank God, is living,
breathing, growing every hour." These words,
delivered from the immortal lips of Benjamin H.
Hill, at Tammany Hall, in 1866, true then and
truer now, I shall make my text to-night.

Mr. President and Gentlemen: Let me ex-
press to you my appreciation of the kindness
by which I am permitted to address you. I
make this abrupt acknowledgment advisedly, for
I feel that if, when I raise my provincial voice in
this ancient and august presence, it could find
courage for no more than the opening sentence, it

Benjamin H. Hill (1823-1882) of Georgia: An
eminent lawyer and statesman.

Tammany Hall: The headquarters of the Democratic party in New York city. Tamenund, or St.
Tammany as he is popularly called, was an Indian
chief who has been adopted as the tutelary genius
of the Democratic party. His motto was, " Unite,—
in peace for prosperity, in war for defence."

23

would be well if in that sentence I had met in a rough sense my obligation as a guest, and had perished, so to speak, with courtesy on my lips and grace in my heart.

Permitted, through your kindness, to catch my second wind, let me say that I appreciate the significance of being the first Southerner to speak at this board, which bears the substance, if it surpasses the semblance, of original New England hospitality — and honors the sentiment that in turn honors you, but in which my personality is lost, and the compliment to my people made plain.

I bespeak the utmost stretch of your courtesy to-night. I am not troubled about those from whom I come. You remember the man whose wife sent him to a neighbor with a pitcher of milk, and who, tripping on the top step, fell with such casual interruptions as the landings afforded into the basement, and, while picking himself up, had the pleasure of hearing his wife call out: " John, did you break the pitcher?"

"No, I didn't," said John, " but I'll be dinged if I don't."

So, while those who call me from behind may inspire me with energy, if not with courage, I ask an indulgent hearing from you. I beg that you will bring your full faith in American fairness and frankness to judgment upon what I shall say. There was an old preacher once who told some boys of the Bible lesson he was going

to read in the morning. The boys, finding the
place, glued together the connecting pages. The
next morning he read on the bottom of one page,
" When Noah was one hundred and twenty years
old he took unto himself a wife, who was "—
then turning the page — " 140 cubits long — 40
cubits wide, built of gopher wood — and covered
with pitch inside and out." He was naturally
puzzled at this. He read it again, verified it, and
then said: " My friends, this is the first time
I ever met this in the Bible, but I accept this as
an evidence of the assertion that we are fearfully
and wonderfully made." If I could get you to
hold such faith to-night I could proceed cheerfully
to the task I otherwise approach with a sense of
consecration.

Pardon me one word, Mr. President, spoken
for the sole purpose of getting into the volumes
that go out annually freighted with the rich eloquence of your speakers — the fact that the Cavalier as well as the Puritan, was on the continent
in its early days, and that he was " up and able
to be about." I have read your books carefully
and I find no mention of the fact, which seems
to me an important one for preserving a sort of
historical equilibrium, if for nothing else.

Let me remind you that the Virginia Cavalier

The Virginia Cavalier first challenged France, &c.:
In the sixteenth and seventeenth centuries the
French explored the vast region from Newfoundland

first challenged France on the continent — that
Cavalier, John Smith, gave New England its
very name, and was so pleased with the job that
he has been handing his own name around ever
since — and that while Myles Standish was cutting off men's ears for courting a girl without
her parents' consent, and forbade men to kiss
their wives on Sunday, the Cavalier was courting
everything in sight, and that the Almighty had
vouchsafed great increase to the Cavalier col-

to Texas, and established here and there rude set-
tlements. Although England claimed the northern
part of the continent by virtue of Cabot's discov-
eries, she did little during the sixteenth century to
make good this claim. In 1607 the first permanent
English settlement in America was made at Jamestown in Virginia, and this little colony was saved
from ruin by Captain John Smith. In 1614 Captain
Smith explored the coast from Penobscot to Cape
Cod and called the country New England.

Myles Standish, &c.: Captain Standish (1584-
1656) was an English officer who emigrated to New
England, and became the military leader of the
colonists in their wars against the Indians. The
laws, especially those about the observance of Sunday, were extremely strict among the Puritan set-
tlers of New England. . Every door was opened
at tap of drum, and men, women, and children
marched to the meeting-house to listen to a sermon
three or four hours long. A man was whipped for
splitting kindling on Sunday to start his fire, or for
chewing tobacco oftener than once a day or within
ten miles of a house.

onies, the huts in the wilderness being as full as the nests in the woods.

But having incorporated the Cavalier as a fact in your charming little books, I shall let him work out his own salvation, as he has always done, with engaging gallantry, and we will hold no controversy as to his merits. Why should we? Neither Puritan nor Cavalier long survived as such. The virtues and good traditions of both happily still live for the inspiration of their sons and the saving of the old fashion. But both Puritan and Cavalier were lost in the storm of the first Revolution, and the American citizen, supplanting both and stronger than either, took possession of the republic bought by their common blood and fashioned to wisdom, and charged himself with teaching men government and establishing the voice of the people as the voice of God.

My friends, Dr. Talmage has told you that the typical American has yet to come. Let me tell you that he has already come. Great types, like valuable plants, are slow to flower and fruit. But from the union of these colonists, Puritans and Cavaliers, from the straightening of their purposes and the crossing of their blood, slow perfecting through a century, came he who stands as the first typical American, the first who

Thomas De Witt Talmage, D. D. (1832-1902) of New Jersey: A popular pulpit orator and lecturer.

comprehended within himself all the strength and gentleness, all the majesty and grace of this republic — Abraham Lincoln. He was the sum of Puritan and Cavalier, for in his ardent nature were fused the virtues of both, and in the depths of his great soul the faults of both were 'lost. He was greater than Puritan, greater than Cavalier, in that he was American, and that in his honest form were first gathered the vast and thrilling forces of his ideal government — charging it with such tremendous meaning and elevating it above human suffering that martyrdom, though infamously aimed, came as a fitting crown to a life consecrated from the cradle to human liberty. Let us, each cherishing the traditions and honoring his fathers, build with reverent hands to the type of this simple but sublime life, in which all types are honored, and in our common glory as Americans there will be plenty and to spare for your forefathers and for mine.

Dr. Talmage has drawn for you, with a master's hand, the picture of your returning armies. He has told you how, in the pomp and circumstance of war, they came back to you, marching with proud and victorious tread, reading their glory in a nation's eyes! Will you bear with me while I tell you of another army that sought its home at the close of the late war — an army that marched home in defeat and not in victory — in pathos and not in splendor, but in glory that equaled yours, and to hearts as loving as ever welcomed heroes home!

Let me picture to you the footsore Confederate soldier, as buttoning up in his faded gray jacket the parole which was to bear testimony to his children of his fidelity and faith, he turned his face southward from Appomattox in April, 1865. Think of him as ragged, half-starved, heavy-hearted, enfeebled by want and wounds, having fought to exhaustion, he surrenders his gun, wrings the hands of his comrades in silence, and lifting his tear-stained and pallid face for the last time to the graves that dot old Virginia hills, pulls his gray cap over his brow and begins the slow and painful journey.

What does he find — let me ask you who went to your homes eager to find, in the welcome you had justly earned, full payment for four years' sacrifice — what does he find when, having fol-lowed the battle-stained cross against overwhelm-

From Appomattox: At Appomattox Court House in Virginia General Lee surrendered to General Grant, April 9, 1865, virtually ending the War between the States.

Battle-stained cross: The Confederate battle flag showed on a red ground a blue cross bearing thirteen white stars. This flag was designed by General Beauregard and was adopted after the first battle of Manassas because, in the smoke of battle, the "stars and bars," the first flag of the Confederacy, was several times mistaken for the "stars and stripes," and *vice versa*.

ing odds, dreading death not half so much as surrender, he reaches the home he left so prosperous and beautiful? He finds his house in ruins, his farm devastated, his slaves free, his stock killed, his barns empty, his trade destroyed, his money worthless, his social system, feudal in its magnificence, swept away; his people without law or legal status; his comrades slain, and the burdens of others heavy on his shoulders. Crushed by defeat, his very traditions are gone. Without money, credit, employment, material, or training; and beside all this, confronted with the gravest problem that ever met human intelligence — the establishment of a status for the vast body of his liberated slaves.

What does he do — this hero in gray with a heart of gold? Does he sit down in sullenness and despair? Not for a day. Surely God, who had stripped him of his prosperity, inspired him in his adversity. As ruin was never before so overwhelming, never was restoration swifter.

The soldier stepped from the trenches into the furrow; horses that had charged Federal guns marched before the plow, and fields that ran red with human blood in April were green with the harvest in June; women reared in luxury cut up their dresses and made breeches for their hus-

Devastated: Laid waste; ravaged.
Status: Standing; condition.

bands, and, with a patience and heroism that fit women always as a garment, gave their hands to work. There was little bitterness in all this. Cheerfulness and frankness prevailed. "Bill Arp" struck the key-note when he said: "Well, I killed as many of them as they did of me, and now I'm going to work." So did the soldier returning home after defeat and roasting some corn on the roadside who made the remark to his comrades: "You may leave the South if you want to, but I'm going to Sandersville, kiss my wife and raise a crop, and if the Yankees fool with me any more, I'll whip 'em again."

I want to say to General Sherman, who is considered an able man in our parts, though some

"**Bill Arp**" (*Bill, A Rebel Private*): The pen-name of Major Charles H. Smith (1826-1903) of Georgia, a popular Southern humorist, the author of "From the Uncivil War to Date," and other books.

General Sherman, &c.: General William Tecumseh Sherman (1820-1891) of Ohio, was a Union general who commanded the Division of the Mississippi in the War between the States. With an army of over a hundred thousand men he marched from Chattanooga, Tenn., to Atlanta, Ga. He burned the city and made his famous march to the sea, laying waste the country from Atlanta to Savannah. Thence he marched to Charleston and to Raleigh. General Sherman reported that on this march through Georgia he used for his army property worth twenty million dollars and destroyed property to the value of eighty millions more.

people think he is a kind of careless man about fire, that from the ashes he left us in 1864 we have raised a brave and beautiful city; that somehow or other we have caught the sunshine in the bricks and mortar of our homes, and have builded therein not one ignoble prejudice or memory.

But what is the sum of our work? We have found out that in the summing up the free negro counts more than he did as a slave. We have planted the schoolhouse on the hilltop and made it free to white and black. We have sowed towns and cities in the place of theories, and put business above politics. We have challenged your spinners in Massachusetts and your ironmakers in Pennsylvania. We have learned that the $400,000,000 annually received from our cotton crop will make us rich when the supplies that make it are home-raised. We have reduced the commercial rate of interest from 24 to 6 per cent., and are floating 4 per cent. bonds. We have learned that one Northern immigrant is worth fifty foreigners and have smoothed the path to Southward, wiped out the place where Mason and Dixon's line used to be, and hung out the latchstring to you and yours.

Mason's and Dixon's line: In 1767 two surveyors named Mason and Dixon fixed the boundary line between Pennsylvania and Maryland. This line became famous as the boundary between the free states of the North and what were the slave-holding states of the South.

We have reached the point that marks perfect
harmony in every household, when the husband
confesses that the pies which his wife cooks are as
good as those his mother used to bake; and we
admit that the sun shines as brightly and the moon
as softly as it did before the war. We have established thrift in city and country. We have fallen
in love with work. We have restored comfort
to homes from which culture and elegance never
departed. We have let economy take root and
spread among us as rank as the crab-grass which
sprung from Sherman's cavalry camps, until we
are ready to lay odds on the Georgia Yankee as
he manufactures relics of the battlefield in a one-
story shanty and squeezes pure olive-oil out of
his cottonseed, against any down-easter that ever
swapped wooden nutmegs for flannel sausage in
the valleys of Vermont. Above all, we know that
we have achieved in these "piping times of
peace" a fuller independence for the South than
that which our fathers sought to win in the forum
by their eloquence or compel in the field by their
swords.

It is a rare privilege, sir, to have had part,
however humble, in this work. Never was
nobler duty confided to human hands than the
uplifting and upbuilding of the prostrate and
bleeding South — misguided, perhaps, but beautiful in her suffering, and honest, brave, and generous always. In the record of her social, indus-

trial, and political illustration we await with confidence the verdict of the world.

But what of the negro? Have we solved the problem he presents or progressed in honor and equity toward solution? Let the record speak to the point. No section shows a more prosperous laboring population than the negroes of the South, none in fuller sympathy with the employing and land-owning class. He shares our school fund, has the fullest protection of our laws and the friendship of our people. Self-interest, as well as honor, demand that he should have this. Our future, our very existence depend upon our working out this problem in full and exact justice. We understand that when Lincoln signed the emancipation proclamation, your victory was assured, for he then committed you to the cause of human liberty, against which the arms of man cannot prevail — while those of our statesmen who trusted to make slavery the cornerstone of the Confederacy doomed us to defeat as far as they could, committing us to a cause that reason could not defend or the sword maintain in sight of advancing civilization.

Had Mr. Toombs said, which he did not say, " that he would call the roll of his slaves at the foot of Bunker Hill," he would have been foolish,

Robert Toombs (1810-1885) of Georgia: An able politician, leader of the secession party in his native state.

for he might have known that whenever slavery became entangled in war it must perish, and that the chattel in human flesh ended forever in New England when your fathers — not to be blamed for parting with what didn't pay — sold their slaves to our fathers — not to be praised for knowing a paying thing when they saw it. The relations of the Southern people with the negro are close and cordial. We remember with what fidelity for four years he guarded our defenseless women and children, whose husbands and fathers were fighting against his freedom. To his eternal credit be it said that whenever he struck a blow for his own liberty he fought in open battle, and when at last he raised his black and humble hands that the shackles might be struck off, those hands were innocent of wrong against his helpless charges, and worthy to be taken in loving grasp by every man who honors loyalty and devotion. Ruffians have maltreated him, rascals have misled him, philanthropists established a bank for him, but the South, with the North, protests against injustice to this simple and sincere people.

To liberty and enfranchisement is as far as law can carry the negro. The rest must be left to conscience and common sense. It must

Chattel: A law term applied to real and personal property. The word is from the Old English *catel,* goods, cattle, because the first property was in cattle.

be left to those among whom his lot is cast, with whom he is indissolubly connected, and whose prosperity depends upon their possessing his intelligent sympathy and confidence. Faith has been kept with him, in spite of calumnious assertions to the contrary by those who assume to speak for us or by frank opponents. Faith will be kept with him in the future, if the South holds her reason and integrity.

But have we kept faith with you? In the fullest sense, yes. When Lee surrendered — I don't say when Johnston surrendered, because I understand he still alludes to the time when he met General Sherman last as the time when he determined to abandon any further prosecution of the struggle — when Lee surrendered, I say, and Johnston quit, the South became and has

Those who assume, &c.: Mr. Grady said that he here referred to the novelist, George W. Cable, and to others whose expressions about Southern affairs and sentiments he regarded as misrepresentations of the most misleading and injurious kind.

Lee surrendered, &c.: The terms offered by General Sherman to the Confederate general, Joseph E. Johnston were considered too liberal by President Lincoln and his cabinet. April 26, 1865, General Johnston surrendered on the same terms that were extended General Lee by General Grant. General Johnston was an able officer who has not increased his reputation by his strictures on the civil and military leaders of the government with which he was identified.

since been, loyal to this Union. We fought hard enough to know that we were whipped, and in perfect frankness accept as final the arbitrament of the sword to which we had appealed. The South found her jewel in the toad's head of defeat. The shackles that had held her in narrow limitations fell forever when the shackles of the negro slave were broken. Under the old regime the negroes were slaves to the South; the South was a slave to the system. The old plantation, with its simple police regulations and feudal habit, was the only type possible under slavery. Thus was gathered in the hands of a splendid and chivalric oligarchy the substance that should have been diffused among the people, as the rich blood, under certain artificial conditions is gathered at the heart, filling that with affluent rapture but leaving the body chill and colorless.

/The old South rested everything on slavery and agriculture, unconscious that these could neither give nor maintain healthy growth. The

Arbitrament: Decision; will.

The South found her jewel, &c.:
" Sweet are the uses of adversity,
Which like the toad, ugly and venomous,
Wears yet a precious jewel in his head."— Shakespeare, *As You Like It,* Act II., Scene 1.

Regime: (Fr.) Mode or style of rule; character of government.

Oligarchy: A form of government in which all the power is in the hands of a few people.

new South presents a perfect democracy, the oligarchs leading in the popular movement — a social system compact and closely knitted, less splendid on the surface, but stronger at the core — a hundred farms for every plantation, fifty homes for every palace — and a diversified industry that meets the complex needs of this complex age.

The new South is enamored of her new work. Her soul is stirred with the breath of a new life. The light of a grander day is falling fair on her face. She is thrilling with the consciousness of growing power and prosperity. As she stands upright, full-statured and equal among the people of the earth, breathing the keen air and looking out upon the expanded horizon, she understands that her emancipation came because through the inscrutable wisdom of God her honest purpose was crossed, and her brave armies were beaten.

New South: "It was he (Ben Hill) who named the New South. One of the 'upstarts' said in a speech in New York: 'In answering the toast to the New South, I accept that name in no disparagement to the Old South. Dear to me, sir, is the home of my childhood and the traditions of my people, and not for the glories of New England history from Plymouth Rock all the way, would I surrender the least of these. Never shall I do or say aught to dim the luster of the glory of my ancestors, won in peace and war.' "—Henry W. Grady, Speech at the Augusta Exposition.

This is said in no spirit of time-serving or apology. The South has nothing for which to apologize. She believes that the late struggle between the States was war and not rebellion; revolution and not conspiracy, and that her convictions were as honest as yours. I should be unjust to the dauntless spirit of the South and to my own convictions if I did not make this plain in this presence. The South has nothing to take back.

In my native town of Athens is a monument that crowns its central hill — a plain, white shaft. Deep cut into its shining side is a name dear to me above the names of men — that of a brave and simple man who died in brave and simple faith. Not for all the glories of New England, from Plymouth Rock all the way, would I exchange the heritage he left me in his soldier's death. To the foot of that I shall send my children's children to reverence him who ennobled their name with his heroic blood. But, sir, speaking from the shadow of that memory which I honor as I do nothing else on earth, I say that the cause in which he suffered and for which he gave his life was adjudged by higher and fuller wisdom than his or mine, and I am glad that the omniscient God held the balance of battle in His Almighty hand and that human slavery

Plymouth Rock: With what historical event is this associated?

was swept forever from American soil — that the American Union was saved from the wreck of war.

This message, Mr. President, comes to you from consecrated ground. Every foot of soil about the city in which I live is sacred as a battle-ground of the republic. Every hill that invests it is hallowed to you by the blood of your brothers who died for your victory, and doubly hallowed to us by the blood of those who died hopeless, but undaunted, in defeat — sacred soil to all of us — rich with memories that make us purer and stronger and better — silent but staunch witnesses in its red desolation of the matchless valor of American hearts and the deathless glory of American arms — speaking an eloquent witness in its white peace and prosperity to the indissoluble union of American States and the imperishable brotherhood of the American people.

Now, what answer has New England to this message? Will she permit the prejudice of war to remain in the hearts of the conquerors, when it has died in the hearts of the conquered? Will she transmit this prejudice to the next generation, that in their hearts which never felt the generous ardor of conflict it may perpetuate itself? Will

City in which I live, &c.: Atlanta, the city defended by General Hood and burned by General Sherman.

she withhold, save in strained courtesy, the hand which straight from his soldier's heart Grant offered to Lee at Appomattox? Will she make the vision of a restored and happy people, which gathered above the couch of your dying captain, filling his heart with grace, touching his lips with praise, and glorifying his path to the grave — will she make this vision on which the last sigh of his expiring soul breathed a benediction, a cheat and delusion?

If she does, the South, never abject in asking for comradeship, must accept with dignity its refusal; but if she does not refuse to accept in frankness and sincerity this message of good will and friendship, then will the prophecy of Webster, delivered in this very society forty years ago amid tremendous applause, become true, be verified in its fullest sense, when he said: " Standing hand to hand and clasping hands, we should remain united as we have been for sixty

Vision of a restored, &c.: It was Lincoln's ardent wish to restore good-will with peace and to re-establish the seceded states on their old footing. His successor, President Johnson, preferred "to make treason odious " by the anarchy of the reconstruction period.

Daniel Webster (1782-1852) of New Hampshire: A celebrated statesman and orator, the mainspring of whose public life was devotion to the Union, " Liberty and union, now and forever, one and inseparable."

years, citizens of the same country, members of
the same government, united, all united now and
united forever." There have been difficulties,
contentions, and controversies, but I tell you that
in my judgment,

> "Those opened eyes,
> Which like the meteors of a troubled heaven,
> All of one nature, of one substance bred,
> Did lately meet in th' intestine shock,
> Shall now, in mutual well beseeming ranks,
> March all one way."

The South and Her Problems

At the Dallas, Texas, State Fair, on the 26th of October, 1887, Mr. Grady was the orator of the day. He said:

" Who saves his country, saves all things, and all things saved will bless him. Who lets his country die, lets all things die, and all things dying curse him."

These words are graven on the statue of Benjamin H. Hill in the city of Atlanta, and in their spirit I shall speak to you to-day.

Mr. President and Fellow-Citizens: I salute the first city of the grandest State of the greatest government on this earth. In paying earnest compliment to this thriving city and this generous multitude, I need not cumber speech with argument or statistics. It is enough to say that my friends and myself make obeisance this morning to the chief metropolis of the State of Texas. If it but holds this pre-eminence — and who can doubt in this auspicious presence that it will — the uprising tides of Texas's prosperity will carry it to glories unspeakable. For I say in soberness, the future of this marvelous and amazing empire, that gives broader and deeper significance to

43

statehood by accepting its modest naming, the mind of man can neither measure nor comprehend.

I shall be pardoned for resisting the inspiration of this presence and adhering to-day to blunt and vigorous speech — for there are times when fine words are paltry, and this seems to me to be such a time. So I shall turn away from the thunders of the political battle upon which every American hangs intent, and repress the ardor that at this time rises in every American heart — for there are issues that strike deeper than any political theory has reached, and conditions of which partisanry has taken, and can take, but little account. Let me, therefore, with studied plainness, and with such precision as is possible — in a spirit of fraternity that is broader than party limitations, and deeper than political motives — discuss with you certain problems upon the wise and prompt solution of which depends the glory and prosperity of the South.

But why — for let us make our way slowly — why " the South." In an indivisible union — in a republic against the integrity of which sword shall never be drawn or mortal hand uplifted, and in which the rich blood gathering at the common heart is sent throbbing into every part of the body politic — why is one section held separated from the rest in alien consideration? We can understand why this should be so in a city that has a community of local interests; or in a State still clothed in that sovereignty of which the debates of peace and the storm of war has not stripped her. But why should a number of States, stretching from Richmond to Galveston, bound together by no local interests, held in no autonomy, be thus combined and drawn to a common center? That man would be absurd who declaimed in Buffalo against the wrongs of the Middle States, or who demanded in Chicago a convention for the West to consider the needs of that section.

If then it be provincialism that holds the South together, let us outgrow it; if it be sectionalism, let us root it out of our hearts; but if it be something deeper than these and essential to our system, let us declare it with frankness, consider it with respect, defend it with firmness, and in dignity abide its consequence. What is it that holds the Southern States — though true in thought and deed to the Union — so closely bound in sympathy to-day? For a century these States championed a governmental theory, but that, having triumphed in every forum, fell at last by the sword. They maintained an institution — but that, having been administered in the fullest wisdom of man, fell at last in the higher wisdom of God. They fought a war — but the prejudices of that war have died, its sympathies

Autonomy: Self government.

have broadened, and its memories are already
the priceless treasure of the republic that is ce-
mented forever with its blood. They looked out
together upon the ashes of their homes and the
desolation of their fields — but out of pitiful resource they have fashioned their homes anew,
and plenty rides on the springing harvests. In
all the past there is nothing to draw them into
essential or lasting alliance — nothing in all that
heroic record that can not be rendered unfearing
from provincial hands into the keeping of American history.

But the future holds a problem, in solving
which the South must stand alone; in dealing
with which, she must come closer together than
ambition or despair have driven her, and on the
outcome of which her very existence depends.
This problem is to carry within her body politic
two separate races, and nearly equal in numbers.
She must carry these races in peace — for dis-
cord means ruin. She must carry them sepa-
rately — for assimilation means debasement.
She must carry them in equal justice — for to
this she is pledged in honor and in gratitude. She
must carry them even unto the end, for in human
probability she will never be quit of either.

This burden no other people bears to-day —
on none hath it ever rested. Without precedent
or companionship, the South must bear this problem, the awful responsibility of which should

win the sympathy of all human kind, and the
protecting watchfulness of God — alone, even
unto the end. Set by this problem apart from
all other peoples of the earth, and her unique
position emphasized rather than relieved, as I
shall show hereafter, by her material conditions,
it is not only fit, but it is essential that she should
hold her brotherhood unimpaired, quicken her
sympathies, and in the lights or in the shadows
of this surpassing problem work out her own salvation in the fear of God — but of God alone.

What shall the South do to be saved? Through
what paths shall she reach the end? Through
what travail, or what splendors, shall she give
to the Union this section, its wealth garnered,
its resources utilized, and its rehabilitation complete — and restore to the world this problem
solved in such justice as the finite mind can
measure, or finite hands administer?

In dealing with this I shall dwell on two
points.

First, the duty of the South in its relation to
the race problem.

Second, the duty of the South in relation to
its no less unique and important industrial problem.

I approach this discussion with a sense of consecration. I beg your patient and cordial sympathy. And I invoke the Almighty God, that
having showered on this people His fullest riches,

has put their hands to this task, that He will draw near unto us, as He drew near to troubled Israel, and lead us in the ways of honor and up-rightness, even through a pillar of cloud by day, and a pillar of fire by night.

What of the negro? This of him. I want no better friend than the black boy who was raised by my side, and who is now trudging pa-tiently with downcast eyes and shambling figure through his lowly way in life. I want no sweeter music than the crooning of my old " mammy," now dead and gone to rest, as I heard it when she held me in her loving arms, and bending her old black face above me stole the cares from my brain, and led me smiling into sleep. I want no truer soul than that which moved the trusty slave, who for four years while my father fought with the armies that barred his freedom, slept every night at my mother's chamber door, hold-ing her and her children as safe as if her hus-band stood guard, and ready to lay down his humble life on her threshold.

History has no parallel to the faith kept by the negro in the South during the war. Often five hundred negroes to a single white man, and yet through these dusky throngs the women and children walked in safety, and the unprotected homes rested in peace. Unmarshaled the black

Pillar of cloud: See Exodus xiii, 21, 22.

battalions moved patiently to the fields in the morning to feed the armies their idleness would have starved, and at night gathered anxiously at the big house to " hear the news from marster," though conscious that his victory made their chains enduring. Everywhere humble and kindly ; the bodyguard of the helpless ; the rough companion of the little ones ; the observant friend ; the silent sentry in his lowly cabin ; the shrewd counselor. And when the dead came home, a mourner at the open grave. A thousand torches would have disbanded every Southern army, but not one was lighted. When the master going to a war in which slavery was involved said to his slave, " I leave my home and loved ones in your charge," the tenderness between man and master stood disclosed. And when the slave held that charge sacred through storm and temptation, he gave new meaning to faith and loyalty. I rejoice that when freedom came to him after years of waiting, it was all the sweeter because the black hands from which the shackles fell were stainless of a single crime against the helpless ones confided to his care.

From this root, imbedded in a century of kind and constant companionship, has sprung some foliage. As no race had ever lived in such unre-

Battalions: Literally, bodies of troops arrayed for battle

sisting bondage, none was ever hurried with such
swiftness through freedom into power. Into
hands still trembling from the blow that broke
the shackles, was thrust the ballot. In less than
twelve months from the day he walked down the
furrow a slave, a negro dictated in legislative
halls from which Davis and Calhoun had gone
forth, the policy of twelve commonwealths.
When his late master protested against his misrule, the federal drum-beat rolled around his
strongholds, and from a hedge of federal bayonets
he grinned in good-natured insolence. From the
proven incapacity of that day has he far ad-
vanced? Simple, credulous, impulsive — easily
led and too often easily bought, is he a safer, more
intelligent citizen now than then? Is this mass of
votes, loosed from old restraints, inviting alliance
or awaiting opportunity, less menacing than when
its purpose was plain and its way direct?

My countrymen, right here the South must
make a decision on which very much depends.
Many wise men hold that the white vote of the
South should divide, the color line be beaten

Twelve Commonwealths: The States of the Confederacy, South Carolina, Mississippi, Florida, Alabama, Georgia, Louisiana, Texas, Virginia, Arkansas,
North Carolina, Tennessee. Missouri, often counted,
passed an ordinance of secession which was never
ratified by the people. Kentucky had representatives in the Confederate Congress and furnished
soldiers to the South.

down, and the Southern States ranged on economic or moral questions as interest or belief demands. I am compelled to dissent from this view. The worst thing, in my opinion, that could happen is that the white people of the South should stand in opposing factions, with the vast mass of ignorant or purchasable negro votes between. Consider such a status. If the negroes were skilfully led — and leaders would not be lacking — it would give them the balance of power — a thing not to be considered. If their vote was not compacted, it would invite the debauching bid of factions, and drift surely to that which was the most corrupt and cunning. With the shiftless habit and irresolution of slavery days still possessing him, the negro voter will not in this generation, adrift from war issues, become a steadfast partisan through conscience or conviction. In every community there are colored men who redeem their race from this reproach, and who vote under reason. Perhaps in time the bulk of this race may thus adjust itself. But, through what long and monstrous periods of political debauchery this status would be reached, no tongue can tell.

The clear and unmistakable domination of the white race, dominating not through violence, not through party alliance, but through the integrity of its own vote and the largeness of its sympathy and justice through which it shall compel the

support of the better classes of the colored race
— that is the hope and assurance of the South.
Otherwise, the negro would be bandied from
one faction to another. His credulity would be
played upon, his cupidity tempted, his impulses
misdirected, his passions inflamed. He would
be forever in alliance with that faction which was
most desperate and unscrupulous. Such a state
would be worse than reconstruction, for then intelligence was banded, and its speedy triumph assured. But with intelligence and property divided — bidding and overbidding for place and
patronage — irritation increasing with each conflict — the bitterness and desperation seizing
every heart — political debauchery deepening, as
each faction staked its all in the miserable game
— there would be no end to this, until our suffrage was hopelessly sullied, our people forever
divided, and our most sacred rights surrendered.

One thing further should be said in perfect
frankness. Up to this point we have dealt with
ignorance and corruption — but beyond this point
a deeper issue confronts us. Ignorance may
struggle to enlightenment, out of corruption may
come the incorruptible. God speed the day when
— every true man will work and pray for its

Reconstruction: The period after the close of
the war during which the governments of the se-
ceding states were set aside and the states were
ruled as conquered provinces.

coming — the negro must be led to know and
through sympathy to confess that his interests
and the interests of the people of the South are
identical. The men who, from afar off, view this
subject through the cold eye of speculation or see
it distorted through partisan glasses insist that
directly or indirectly the negro race shall be in
control of the affairs of the South. We have no
fears of this; already we are attracting to us the
best elements of the race, and as we proceed our
alliance will broaden; external pressure but irri-
tates and impedes. Those who would put the
negro race in supremacy would work against in-
fallible decree, for the white race can never submit to its domination, because the white race is
the superior race. But the supremacy of the
white race of the South must be maintained forever, and the domination of the negro race re-
sisted at all points and at all hazards — because
the white race is the superior race. This is the
declaration of no new truth. It has abided forever in the marrow of our bones, and shall run
forever with the blood that feeds Anglo-Saxon
hearts.

In political compliance the South has evaded
the truth, and men have drifted from their convictions. But we can not escape this issue. It
faces us wherever we turn. It is an issue that
has been, and will be. The races and tribes of
earth are of divine origin. Behind the laws of

man and the decrees of war, stands the law of
God. What God hath separated let no man join
together. The Indian, the Malay, the Negro, the
Caucasian, these types stand as markers of God's
will. Let no man tinker with the work of the
Almighty. Unity of civilization, no more than
unity of faith, will never be witnessed on earth.
No race has risen, or will rise, above its ordained
place. Here is the pivotal fact of this great
matter — two races are made equal in law, and
in political rights, between whom the ·caste of
race has set an impassable gulf. This gulf is
bridged by a statute, and the races are urged to
cross thereon. This cannot be. The fiat of the
Almighty has gone forth, and in eighteen centuries of history it is written.

We would escape this issue if we could. From
the depths of its soul the South invokes from
heaven " peace on earth, and good will to man."
She would not, if she could, cast this race back
into the condition from which it was righteously
raised. She would not deny its smallest ·or

Caste of race: The Hindoos have for unrecorded
centuries been divided into castes, or classes, between which there is no social intercourse. Racial
differences constitute castes between which there
is a gulf more impassable than the law and cus-
toms of the Hindoos.

Bridged by a statute: The Fourteenth Amend-
ment to the Constitution.

Fiat: Decisive command; decree.

abridge its fullest privilege. Not to lift this burden forever from her people would she do the least of these things. She must walk through the valley of the shadow, for God has so ordained. But He has ordained that she shall walk in that integrity of race that was created in His wisdom and has been perpetuated in His strength. Standing in the presence of this multitude, sobered with the responsibility of the message I deliver to the young men of the South, I declare that the truth above all others to be worn unsullied and sacred in your hearts, to be surrendered to no force, sold for no price, compromised in no necessity, but cherished and defended as the covenant of your prosperity, and the pledge of peace to your children, is that the white race must dominate forever in the South, because it is the white race, and superior to that race by which its supremacy is threatened.

It is a race issue. Let us come to this point, and stand here. Here the air is pure and the light is clear, and here honor and peace abide. Juggling and evasion deceive not a man. Compromise and subservience have carried not a point. There is not a white man North or South who does not feel it stir in the gray matter of his brain and throb in his heart, not a negro who does not feel its power. It is not a sectional

Subservience: Service in an inferior capacity.

issue. It speaks in Ohio and in Georgia. It speaks wherever the Anglo-Saxon touches an alien race. It has just spoken in universally approved legislation in excluding the Chinaman from our gates, not for his ignorance, vice, or corruption, but because he sought to establish an inferior race in a republic fashioned in the wisdom and defended by the blood of a homogeneous people.

The Anglo-Saxon blood has dominated always and everywhere. It fed Alfred when he wrote the charter of English liberty; it gathered about Hampden as he stood beneath the oak; it thundered in Cromwell's veins as he fought his

Excluding the Chinaman: A treaty with China in 1880 gave the United States the right to regulate Chinese immigration, and this right was exercised by the passing of the Chinese Immigration Act. It shut out the Chinese cheap labor, which was regarded with disfavor by the laborers of the Pacific slope.

Homogeneous: Of the same kind, nature, or race.

Alfred the Great (848-901): One of the Saxon kings of England who worked for the material and intellectual upbuilding of his country. After freeing England from Danish invaders, he established a thorough administration of justice.

John Hampden (1594-1642): A famous English patriot and statesman who defended the cause of the people against the oppression of Charles I.; and

Oliver Cromwell (1599-1658): Leader of English armies and Lord Protector of the Commonwealth established after the execution of Charles I., 1649.

king; it humbled Napoleon at Waterloo; it has
touched the desert and jungle with undying
glory; it carried the drumbeat of England around
the world and spread on every continent the gospel of liberty and of God; it established this republic, carved it from the wilderness, conquered
it from the Indians, wrested it from England,
and at last, stilling its own tumult, consecrated
it forever as the home of the Anglo-Saxon, and
the theater of his transcending achievement.
Never one foot of it can be surrendered, while
that blood lives in American veins and feeds
American hearts, to the domination of an alien
and inferior race.

And yet that is just what is proposed. Not
in twenty years have we seen a day so pregnant
with fate to this section as the sixth of next
November. If President Cleveland is then defeated, which God forbid, I believe these States
will be led through sorrows compared to which
the woes of reconstruction will be as the fading
dews of morning to the roaring flood. To dominate these States through the colored vote, with
such aid as federal patronage may debauch or

Napoleon Bonaparte (1769-1821): A Corsican
general who became emperor of the French. The
greatest general of modern times, he made himself
master of the world, but his despotism led the
powers of Europe to unite against him and he was
overthrown in the battle of Waterloo, 1815.

federal power determine, and thus through its chosen instruments perpetuate its rule, is in my opinion the settled purpose of the Republican party. I am appalled when I measure the passion in which this negro problem is judged by the leaders of the party.

Fifteen years ago Vice-President Wilson said —and I honor his memory as that of a courageous man: " We shall not have finished with the South until we force its people to change their thought, and think as we think." I repeat these words, for I heard them when a boy, and they fell on my ears as the knell of my people's rights —" to change their thought, and make them think as we think." Not enough to have conquered our armies — to have decimated our ranks, to have desolated our fields and reduced us to poverty, to have struck the ballot from our hands and enfranchised our slaves — to have held us prostrate under bayonets while the insolent mocked and thieves plundered — but their very souls must be rifled of their faiths, their sacred traditions cudgeled from memory, and their immortal minds

Vice President Henry Wilson (1812-1875) of New Hampshire: He served with President Grant in his second term, before the close of which Wilson died.

Decimated: Literally, selected by lot and punished with death every tenth man of a body of men; destroyed a great part of.

beaten into subjection until thought had lost its
integrity, and we were forced " to think as they
think."

And just now General Sherman has said, and I
honor him as a soldier: " The negro must be
allowed to vote, and his vote must be counted;
otherwise, so sure as there is a God in heaven,
you will have another war, more cruel than the
last, when the torch and dagger will take the place
of the muskets of well-ordered battalions. Should
the negro strike that blow, in seeming justice,
there will be millions to assist them."

And this General took Johnston's sword in
surrender! He looked upon the thin and ragged
battalions in gray, that for four years had held
his teeming and heroic legions at bay. Facing
them, he read their courage in their depleted
ranks and gave them a soldier's parole. When
he found it in his heart to taunt these heroes with
this threat, why — careless as he was twenty
years ago with fire, he is even more careless now
with his words. If we could hope that this problem would be settled within our lives I would appeal from neither madness nor unmanliness. But
when I know that, strive as I may, I must at last
render this awful heritage into the untried hands
of my son, already dearer to me than my life,
and that he must in turn bequeath it unsolved to
his children, I cry out against the inhumanity
that deepens its difficulties with this incendiary

threat and beclouds its real issue with inflaming passion.

This problem is not only enduring, but it is widening. The exclusion of the Chinese is the first step in the revolution that shall save liberty and law and religion to this land, and in peace and order, not enforced on the gallows or at the bayonet's end, but proceeding from the heart of an harmonious people, shall secure in the enjoyment of the rights and the control of this republic, the homogeneous people that established and has maintained it.

The next step will be taken when some brave statesman, looking Demagogy in the face, shall move to call to the stranger at our gates, " Who comes there?" admitting every man who seeks a home or honors our institutions and whose habit and blood will run with the native current; but excluding all who seek to plant anarchy or to establish alien men or measures on our soil; and will then demand that the standard of our citizenship be lifted and the right of acquiring our suffrage be abridged. When that day comes, and God speed its coming, the position of the South will be fully understood and everywhere approved. Until then, let us — giving the negro every right, civil and political,

Demagogy: The arts and practices of a demagogue, a leader who controls the people, especially by deceit and appeals to prejudice and passions.

measured in that fullness the strong should always accord the weak — holding him in closer
friendship and sympathy than he is held by
those who would crucify us for his sake — realiz-
ing that on his prosperity ours depends — let us
resolve that never by external pressure, or in-
ternal division, shall he establish domination,
directly or indirectly, over that race that everywhere has maintained its supremacy. Let this
resolution be cast on the lines of equity and justice. Let it be the pledge of honest, safe, and im-
partial administration, and we shall command
the support of the colored race itself, more dependent than any other on the bounty and pro
tection of government. Let us be wise and patient, and we shall secure through its acqui-
escence what otherwise we should win through
conflict and hold in insecurity.

All this is no unkindness to the negro — but
rather that he may be led in equal rights and
in peace to his uttermost good. Not in sectionalism — for my heart beats true to the Union,
to the glory of which your life and heart is
pledged. Not in disregard of the world's opinion — for to render back this problem in the
world's approval is the sum of my ambition and
the height of human achievement. Not in re-
actionary spirit — but rather to make clear that
new and grander way up which the South is
marching to higher destiny, and on which I

would not halt her for all the spoils that have
been gathered unto parties since Catiline conspired and Cæsar fought. Not in passion, my
countrymen, but in reason — not in narrowness
but in breadth — that we may solve this problem in calmness and in truth, and lifting its
shadows let perpetual sunshine pour down on
two races, walking together in peace and contentment. Then shall this problem have proved our
blessing, and the race that threatened our ruin
work our salvation as it fills our fields with the
best peasantry the world has ever seen. Then
the South — putting behind her all the achieve-
ments of her past — and in war and in peace they
beggar eulogy — may stand upright among the
nations and challenge the judgment of man and
the approval of God, in having worked out in
their sympathy, and in His guidance, this last
and surpassing miracle of human government.

What of the South's industrial problem?
When we remember that amazement followed the
payment by thirty-seven million Frenchmen of

Catiline (108-62 B. C.): A Roman demagogue
and conspirator. Defeated in his plan of making
his faction the foremost in Rome, he formed a conspiracy against the republic. Against him the famous orator, Cicero, delivered some of his most
eloquent orations.

Julius Cæsar (100-44 B. C.): One of the greatest of the Roman generals, statesmen, and rulers.
"The world's great master and his own."— Pope

a billion dollars indemnity to Germany, that the five million whites of the South rendered to the torch and sword three billions of property — that thirty million dollars a year, or six hundred million dollars in twenty years, has been given willingly of our poverty as pensions for Northern soldiers, the wonder is that we are here at all.

There is a figure with which history has dealt lightly, but that, standing pathetic and heroic in the genesis of our new growth, has interested me greatly — our soldier farmer of '65. What chance had he for the future as he wandered amid his empty barns, his stock, labor, and implements gone — gathered up the fragments of his wreck —urging kindly his borrowed mule — paying sixty per cent. for all that he bought, and buying all on credit — his crop mortgaged before it was planted — his children in want, his neighborhood in chaos — working under new conditions and retrieving every error by a costly year — plodding all day down the furrow, hopeless and adrift, save when at night he went back to his broken home, where his wife, cheerful even then, renewed his courage, while she ministered to him in loving tenderness. Who would have thought as during those lonely and terrible days he walked behind the plow, locking the sunshine in the glory of his harvest and spreading the showers in the verdure of his

Genesis: Formation; act of originating.

field — no friend near save nature that smiled at
his earnest touch, and God that sent him the message of good cheer through the passing breeze and
the whispering leaves — that he would in twenty
years, having carried these burdens uncomplaining, make a crop of $800,000,000.   Yet this
he has done, and from his bounty the South has
rebuilded her cities, and recouped her losses.
While we exult in his splendid achievement, let
us take account of his standing.

Whence this enormous growth?   For ten years
the world has been at peace.   The pioneer has
now replaced the soldier.   Commerce has whitened new seas, and the merchant has occupied
new areas.   Steam has made of the earth a chess-
board, on which men play for markets.   Our
western wheat-grower competes in London with
the Russian and the East Indian.   The Ohio
wool-grower watches the Australian shepherd,
and the bleat of the now historic sheep of Vermont is answered from the steppes of Asia.   The
herds that emerge from the dust of your amazing prairies might hear in their pauses the hoof-
beats of antipodean herds marching to meet them.
Under Holland's dykes, the cheese and butter
makers fight American dairies.   The hen cackles
around the world.   California challenges vine-

Recouped: Literally, cut again; as a law term, it
means lessened damages by cutting out or keeping
back a part of.

clad France. The dark continent is disclosed through meshes of light. There is competition everywhere. The husbandman, driven from his market, balances price against starvation and undercuts his rival. This conflict often runs to panic, and profit vanishes. The Iowa farmer burning his corn for fuel is not an unusual type.

Amid this universal conflict, where stands the South? While the producer of everything we eat or wear, in every land, is fighting through glutted markets for bare existence, what of the Southern farmer? In his industrial as in his political problem he is set apart — not in doubt, but in assured independence. Cotton makes him king. Not the fleeces that Jason sought can rival the richness of this plant, as it unfurls its banners in our fields. It is gold from the instant it puts forth its tiny shoot. The shower that whispers to it is heard around the world. The trespass of a worm on its green leaf means more to England than the advance of the Russians on her Asiatic outposts. When its fibre, current in every bank, is marketed, it renders back to the South $350,000,000 every year. Its seed will

Dark Continent: Africa.

Jason: A semi-fabulous Greek hero, who led an expedition to get the wonderful golden fleece which was guarded by a dragon. Jason succeeded in his enterprise through the aid of Medea, a sorceress.

It renders back to the South, &c.: " During the last three years the South's cotton and cotton seed yield $60,000,000 worth of oil to the pre,s and $40,000,000 in food for soil and beast, making the stupendous total of $450,000,000 annual income from this crop. And now, under the Tompkins patent, from its stalk newspaper is to be made at two cents per pound. Edward Atkinson once said: " If New England could grow the cotton plant, without lint, it would make her richest crop; if she held monopoly of cotton lint and seed she would control the commerce of the world."

crops have averaged considerably over $500,000,-000 a year, a gain in three years of not less than $400,000,000 compared with the aggregate of the three preceding years. It is safe to estimate that this year's cotton and cotton seed crop will during the coming twelve months bring to the farmers of the South at least $600,000,000, and so great has been the progress in the development of diversified farming, including truck growing and fruit raising for northern and western markets, that other agricultural products of the South will aggregate not far from $900,000,000, or a total of $1,500,000,000 as the outcome of the farming operations of the South this year. In 1900, according to the census report, the value of the agricultural products of the South was $1,271,000,000 against $660,000,000 in 1880."—R. H. Edmonds, Editor and Manager of *The Manufacturer's Record.*

Edward Atkinson (1827): An American economist who has written on the subjects of labor and capital, banking, cotton supply, &c.

But is our monopoly, threatened from Egypt, India, and Brazil, sure and permanent? Let the record answer. In '72 the American supply of cotton was 3,241,000 bales,— foreign supply 3,-036,000. We led our rivals by less than 200,000 bales. This year the American supply is 8,000,-000 bales — from foreign sources, 2,100,000 expressed in bales of four hundred pounds each. In spite of new areas elsewhere, of fuller experience, of better transportation, and unlimited money spent in experiment, the supply of foreign cotton has decreased since '72 nearly 1,000,000 bales, while that of the South has increased nearly 5,000,000. Further than this: Since 1872, population in Europe has increased 13 per cent., and cotton consumption in Europe has increased 50 per cent. Still further: Since 1880 cotton consumption in Europe has increased 28 per cent., wool only 4 per cent., and flax has decreased 11 per cent. As for new areas, the uttermost missionary woos the heathen with a cotton shirt in one hand and a Bible in the other, and no savage I believe has ever been converted to one

The American supply of cotton, &c.: "The world's production of cotton has averaged, for the last six years, 13,470,000 bales of five hundred pounds each, of which the South is now producing an average of 10,023,000 bales, or seventy-five per cent. The South is now producing an average of about 10,500,000 bales a year."— R. H. Edmonds.

without adopting the other. To summarize:
Our American fibre has increased its product
nearly three-fold, while it has seen the product
of its rival decrease one-third. It has enlarged its
dominion in the old centers of population, supplanting flax and wool, and it peeps from the
satchel of every business and religious evangel-
ist that trots the globe. In three years the American crop has increased 1,400,000 bales, and yet
there is less cotton in the world to-day than at
any time for twenty years. The dominion of our
king is established; this princely revenue assured,
not for a year, but for all time. It is the heritage
that God gave us when he arched our skies, established our mountains, girt us about with the
ocean, tempered the sunshine, and measured the
rain — ours and our children's forever.

Not alone in cotton, but in iron, does the
South excel. The Hon. Mr. Norton, who honors
this platform with his presence, once said to me:
" An Englishman of the highest character pre-
dicted that the Atlantic will be whitened within
our lives with sails carrying American iron and
coal to England." When he made that prediction
the English miners were exhausting the coal in
long tunnels above which the ocean thundered.
Having ores and coal stored in exhaustless quantity, in such richness and in such adjustment
that iron can be made and manufacturing done
cheaper than elsewhere on this continent, is to

now command, and at last control, the world's market for iron. The South now sells iron, through Pittsburg, in New York. She has driven Scotch iron first from the interior, and finally from American ports. Within our lives she will cross the Atlantic, and fulfill the Englishman's prophecy. In 1880 the South made 212,000 tons of iron. In 1887, 845,000 tons. She is now actu-

In 1880 the South made, &c.: "The statistics of pig iron production, as published in *The Manufacturer's Record* this week, show a total output in the Southern states for the first half of 1903 of 1,693,-000 tons against 1,458,000 tons for the corresponding period of 1902, a gain of 230,000 tons. On this basis, taking into account several new furnaces lately built, it is safe to count, even allowing for contingencies, that the production during the second half of the year will exceed these figures, thus assuring to the South an output for the year of not less than 3,500,000 tons, nearly one-half of which will be the production of Alabama. In this connection it is interesting to note that in 1880 the total production of pig iron in the South was 390,-000 tons, and that the total production for the entire country in the same year was only 3,800,000 tons, or but little more than the production of the South the present year. In 1880 the output of bituminous coal in the · United States was 42,000,-000 tons, of which 6,000 000 tons were in the South. Last year the South alone mined 61,000,000, which was ten times its output of 1880 and fifty per cent more bituminous coal than the United States mined in 1880. What has been done in coal and iron but illustrates what is being done in the development

ally building, or has finished this year, furnaces
that will produce more than her entire product
of last year. Birmingham alone will produce
more iron in 1889 than the entire South produced
in 1887.

Our coal supply is exhaustless, Texas alone
having 6,000 square miles. In marble and
granite we have no rivals, as to quantity or quality. In lumber our riches are even vaster. More
than fifty per cent. of our entire area is in forests,
making the South the best timbered region in the
world. We have enough merchantable yellow
pine to bring in money, $2,500,000,000 — a sum
the vastness of which can only be understood
when I say it nearly equals the assessed value of
the entire South, including cities, forests, farms,
mines, factories and personal property of every
description whatsoever. Back of this are our
forests of hard woods and measureless swamps
of cypress and gum. Think of it. In cotton a
monopoly. In iron and coal establishing a swift
mastery. In granite and marble developing equal
advantage and resource. In yellow pine and
hard woods the world's treasury. Surely the
basis of the South's wealth and power is laid
by the hand of the Almighty God, and its prosperity has been established by divine law which

of cotton mill interests and nearly all other lines
of manufacturing."— R. H. Edmonds.

works in eternal justice and not by taxes levied on its neighbors through human statutes. Paying tribute for fifty years that under artificial conditions other sections might reach a prosperity impossible under natural laws, it has grown apace — and its growth shall endure if its people are ruled by two maxims, that reach deeper than legislative enactment, and the operation of which can not be limited by artificial restraint and but little hastened by artificial stimulus.

First: No one crop will make a people prosperous. If cotton held its monopoly under conditions that made other crops impossible, or under allurements that made other crops exceptional, its dominion would be despotism.

Whenever the greed for a money crop unbalances the wisdom of husbandry, the money crop is a curse. When it stimulates the general economy of the farm, it is the profit of farming. In an unprosperous strip of Carolina, when asked the cause of their poverty, the people say, " Tobacco — for it is our only crop." In Lancaster, Pa., the richest American county by the census, when asked the cause of their prosperity, they say, " Tobacco — for it is the golden crown of a diversified agriculture." The soil that produces cotton invites the grains and grasses, the orchard and the vine. Clover, corn, cotton, wheat, and barley thrive in the same inclosure; the peach, the apple, the apricot, and the Siberian crab in the same orchard. Herds and flocks graze ten months every year in the meadows over which winter is but a passing breath, and in which spring and autumn meet in summer's heart. Sugar-cane and oats, rice and potatoes, are extremes that come together under our skies. To raise cotton and send its princely revenues to the west for supplies and to the east for usury, would be misfortune if soil and climate forced such a curse. When both invite independence, to remain in slavery is a crime. To mortgage our farms in Boston for money with which to buy meat and bread from western cribs and smoke-houses, is folly unspeakable.

I rejoice that Texas is less open to this charge than others of the cotton States. With her eighty million bushels of grain, and her sixteen million head of stock, she is rapidly learning that diversified agriculture means prosperity. Indeed, the South is rapidly learning the same lesson; and learned through years of debt and dependence it will never be forgotten. The best thing Georgia has done in twenty years was to raise her oat crop in one season from two million to nine million bushels, without losing a bale of her cotton. It is more for the South that she has increased her crop of corn — that best of grains, of which Samuel J. Tilden said, " It will be the staple food of

Samuel Jones Tilden (1814-1886) of New York: An American statesman, the Democratic candidate

the future, and men will be stronger and better when that day comes "— by forty-three million bushels this year, than to have won a pivotal battle in the late war. In this one item she keeps at home this year a sum equal to the entire cotton crop of my State that last year went to the west.

This is the road to prosperity. It is the way to manliness and sturdiness of character. When every farmer in the South shall eat bread from his own fields and meat from his own pastures, and disturbed by no creditor and enslaved by no debt, shall sit among his teeming gardens and orchards and vineyards and dairies and barnyards, pitching his crops in his own wisdom and growing them in independence, making cotton his clean surplus, and selling it in his own time and in his chosen market and not at a master's bidding — getting his pay in cash and not in a receipted mortgage that discharges his debt, but does not restore his freedom — then shall be breaking the fullness of our day.

Great is King Cotton! But to lie at his feet while the usurer and grain-raiser bind us in subjection, is to invite the contempt of man and the

for the presidency of the United States in 1876. His election was disputed by Hayes, to whom the commission, eight Republicans and seven Democrats, appointed by congress, assigned the place by a strictly party vote.

reproach of God.   But to stand up before him, and amid the crops and smokehouses wrest from him the magna charta of our independence, and to establish in his name an ample and diversified agriculture, that shall honor him while it enriches us — this is to carry us as far in the way of happiness and independence as the farmer, working in the fullest wisdom and in the richest field, can carry any people.

But agriculture alone — no matter how rich or varied its resources — cannot establish or maintain a people's prosperity.   There is a lesson in this that Texas may learn with profit.   No commonwealth ever came to greatness by producing raw material.   Less can this be possible in the future than in the past.   The Comstock lode is the richest spot on earth.   And yet the miners, gasping for breath fifteen hundred feet below the earth's surface, get bare existence out of the splendor they dig from the earth.   It goes to carry the commerce and uphold the industry of distant lands, of which the men who produce it get but dim report.   Hardly more is the South profited when, stripping the harvest of her cotton fields or striking her teeming hills or level-

Magna Charta: The great charter obtained by the English barons from King John in 1213; hence, as here, that which guarantees rights and privileges, and asserts freedom.

Comstock Lode: A very rich gold mine in California.

ing her superb forests, she sends her raw material to augment the wealth and power of distant communities.

Texas produces a million and a half bales of cotton, which yield her $60,000,000. That cotton woven into common goods would add $75,000,000 to Texas's income from this crop, and employ 120,000 operatives, who would spend within her borders more than $30,000,000 in wages. Massachusetts manufactures 575,000 bales of cotton, for which she pays $31,000,000, and sells for $72,000,000, adding a value nearly equal to Texas's gross revenue from cotton, and yet Texas has a clean advantage for manufacturing this cotton of one per cent. a pound over Massachusetts.

That cotton woven, &c.: "In 1880 the South had 667,000 spindles, out of a total of 10,768,000, and its capital invested in cotton manufacturing was $21,-000,000 — a fraction over one-tenth of the cotton mill capital of the country. By 1890, the number of spindles had increased to 1,700,000, and the capital to $61,000,000, the capital then being over one-sixth of the total for the country, and the South had then, for the first time, come to be seriously regarded as a possible dominant factor in certain lines of cotton goods. The census of 1900 showed that in that year the South had 4,500,000 active spindles and $112,000,000 of cotton mill capital. At the present time the South has, in round figures, a total of about 8,000,000 spindles, representing an investment of between $175,000,000 and $200,000,000."
—R. H. Edmonds.

The little village of Grand Rapids began manufacturing furniture simply because it was set in a timber district. It is now a great city and sells $10,000,000 worth of furniture every year, in making which 12,500 men are employed, and a population of 40,000 people supported. The best pine districts of the world are in eastern Texas. With less competition and wider markets than Grand Rapids has, will she ship her forests at prices that barely support the woodchopper and sawyer, to be returned in the making of which great cities are built or maintained? When her farmers and herdsmen draw from her cities $126,000,000 as the price of her annual produce, shall this enormous wealth be scattered through distant shops and factories, leaving in the hands of Texas no more than the sustenance, support, and the narrow brokerage between buyer and seller? As one-crop farming cannot support the country, neither can a resource of commercial exchange support a city. Texas wants immigrants — she needs them — for if every human being in Texas were placed at equi-distant points through the State no Texan could hear the sound of a human voice in your broad areas.

So how can you best attract immigration? By furnishing work for the artisan and mechanic if you meet the demand of your population for cheaper and essential manufactured articles. One half million workers would be needed for this,

and with their families would double the population of your State. In these mechanics and
their dependents, farmers would find a market for
not only their staple crops but for the truck that
they now despise to raise or sell, but is at last
the cream of the farm. Worcester county, Mass.,
takes $7,200,000 of our material and turns out
$87,000,000 of products every year paying $20,-
000,000 in wages.

The most prosperous section of this world
is that known as the Middle States of this
republic. With agriculture and manufactures
in the balance, and their shops and factories
set amid rich and ample acres, the result
is such deep and diffuse prosperity as no other
section can show. Suppose those States had a
monopoly of cotton and coal so disposed as to
command the world's markets and the treasury
of the world's timber, I suppose the mind is
staggered in contemplating the majesty of the
wealth and power they would attain. What have
they that the South lacks?— and to her these
things were added, and climate, ampler acres, and
rich soil. It is a curious fact that three-fourths
of the population and manufacturing wealth of
this country is comprised in a narrow strip between Iowa and Massachusetts, comprising less
than one-sixth of our territory, and that this
strip is distant from the source of raw materials
on which its growth is based, of hard climate and

in a large part of sterile soil.   Much of this forced
and unnatural development is due to slavery,
which for a century fenced enterprise and capital out of the South.   Mr. Thomas, who, in the
Lehigh Valley, owned a furnace in 1845 that set
the pattern for iron-making in America, had at
that time bought mines and forests where Birmingham now stands.   Slavery forced him away.
He settled in Pennsylvania.   I have wondered
what would have happened if that one man had
opened his iron mines in Alabama and set his
furnaces there at that time.   I know what is
going to happen since he has been forced to come
to Birmingham and put up two furnaces nearly
forty years after his survey.

Another cause that has prospered New England and the Middle States while the South lan-
guished, is the system of tariff taxes levied on
the unmixed agriculture of these States for the
protection of industries to our neighbors to the
North, a system on which the Hon. Roger Q.
Mills — that lion of the tribe of Judah — has
at last laid his mighty paw and under the indig-
nant touch of which it trembles to its center.
That system is to be revised and its duties reduced, as we all agree it should be, though I

Lion of the tribe of Judah: "Judah is a lion's
whelp: . . . he couches as a lion and as an old lion;
who shall rouse him up?" Genesis xlix., 9.

Roger Q. Mills was a well-known Texan, prominent in Congressional discussions of the tariff.

should say in perfect frankness I do not agree with Mr. Mills in it. Let us hope this will be done with care and industrious patience. Whether it stands or falls, the South has entered the industrial list to partake of its bounty if it stands, and if it falls, to rely on the favor with which nature has endowed her, and from this immutable advantage to fill her own markets and then have a talk with the world at large.

With amazing rapidity she has moved away from the one-crop idea that was once her curse.

With amazing rapidity, &c.: "In 1880 the South had forty mills engaged in the cotton seed oil industry, with $5,500,000 aggregate capital, but the number is now seventy, with $50,000,000 capital, and a yearly product worth $125,000,000.

"New cotton mills in South Carolina, with a capitalization of $1,995,000, have been chartered since August first, 1902. In addition, existing mills increased their capitalization by $3,120,000, making a total increased investment in the cotton industry in this one state of $5,115,000, in a single year.

"Rice culture in Texas employed 200,000 acres in 1893, but now employs 600,000 acres. Two rice mills located in New Orleans in 1893, now seventy-five mills are distributed over the rice belt.

"In the two years 1901-1902, assessed valuation in the South increased $460,000,000, made up as follows:

Alabama	$ 25,727,108
Arkansas	23,358,898
District of Columbia	7,429,426
Florida	6,361,983
Georgia	33,986,955

In 1880 she was esteemed prosperous. Since that time she added 393,000,000 bushels to her grain crops, and 182,000,000 head to her live stock. This has not lost one bale of her cotton crop, which, on the contrary, has increased nearly 200,000 bales. With equal swiftness has she moved away from the folly of shipping out her

Kentucky	51,254,059
Louisiana	38,924,061
Maryland	50,138,021
Mississippi	25,423,179
North Carolina	34,642,294
South Carolina	15,935,294
Tennessee	8,934,883
Texas	103,564,098
Virginia	20,859,751
West Virginia	12,736,671

" The total assessed property valuation of these Southern states by census periods and for 1902 was:

1880	$3,051,175,098
1890	4,659,514,833
1900	5,457,553,031
1902	5,916,960,712

" These figures show that the $460,000,000 gain in the two years 1901-1902 is $62,000,000, more than half the $798,000,000 gain in the ten years 1890-1900.

" The census of 1900 gives the following Southern values:

Farm values	$3,951,631,632
Capital in manufacturing	1,153,002,368
Railroads (estimated)	2,734,888,000
Total	$7,839,522,000

This total shows 36 per cent increase over 1890 census."— W. J. Ballard.

ore at $2 a ton and buying it back in implements
at from $20 to $100 per ton; her cotton at 10
cents a pound, and buying it back in cloth at
20 to 80 cents a pound; her timber at 8 per thousand and buying it back in furniture at ten to
twenty times as much. In the past eight years
$250,000,000 have been invested in new shops
and factories in her States; 225,000 artisans are
now working that eight years ago were idle or
worked elsewhere, and these added $227,000,000
to the value of her raw material — more than
half the value of her cotton. Add to this the
value of her increased grain crops and stock,
and in the past eight years she has grown in her
fields or created in her shops manufactures more
than the value of her cotton crop. The incom-
ing tide has begun to rise. Every train brings
manufacturers from the East and West seeking
to establish themselves or their sons near the
raw material and in this growing market. Let
the fullness of the tide roll in.

It will not exhaust our materials, nor shall we
glut our markets. When the growing demand
of our Southern market, feeding on its own
growth, is met, we shall find new markets for
the South. Under our new condition many in-
direct laws of commerce shall be straightened.
We buy from Brazil $50,000,000 worth of goods,
and sell her $8,500,000. England buys only $29,-
000,000, and sells her $35,000,000. Of $65,000,-

ooo in cotton goods bought by Central and South
America, over $50,000,000 went to England. Of
$331,000,000 sent abroad by the southern half of
our hemisphere, England secures over half, although we buy from that section nearly twice as
much as England. Our neighbors to the South
need nearly every article we make; we need
nearly everything they produce. Less than 2,500
miles of road must be built to bind by rail the two
American continents. When this is done, and
even before, we shall find exhaustless markets
to the South. Texas shall command, as she
stands in the van of this new movement, its richest
rewards.

The South, under the rapid diversification of
crops and diversification of industries, is thrilling
with new life. As this new prosperity comes
to us, it will bring no sweeter thought to me,
and to you, my countrymen, I am sure, than that
it adds not only to the comfort and happiness of
our neighbors, but that it makes broader the glory
and deeper the majesty and more enduring the
strength, of the Union which reigns supreme in
our hearts. In this republic of ours is lodged
the hope of free government on earth. Here
God has rested the ark of his covenant with the
sons of men. Let us — once estranged and there-
by closer bound — let us soar above all provincial
pride and find our deeper inspirations in gathering the fullest sheaves into the harvest and stand-

ing the staunchest and most devoted of its sons as it lights the path and makes clear the way through which all the people of this earth shall come in God's appointed time.

A few words to the young men of Texas. I am glad that I can speak to them at all. Men, especially young men, look back for their inspirations to what is best in their traditions. Thermopylæ cast Spartan sentiment in heroic mould and sustained Spartan arms for more than a century. Thermopylæ had survivors to tell the story of its defeat. The Alamo had none. Though voiceless it shall speak from its dumb walls. Liberty cried out to Texas, as God called from the clouds unto Moses. Bowie and Fannin, though

Thermopylæ: A narrow pass in Greece where three hundred Spartan soldiers, rather than retreat, died before a mighty army of invading Persians under Xerxes.

Alamo: Texas was originally part of Mexico. Many Americans settled in Texas, became dissatisfied with the Mexican government and declared their independence in 1835. Santa Anna, the Mexican general, entered Texas with a large force and attacked the Alamo, a mission building in San Antonio, which was defended by about two hundred Texans. After a siege of two weeks, the few survivors of this small force surrendered under promise of honorable treatment, but every man was massacred.

James Bowie: A famous Southern frontierman (1790-1836), inventor of the knife named after him. He fell in the Texan War.

Col. James W. Fannin of North Carolina: An offi-

dead, still live. Their voices rang above the din of Goliad and the glory of San Jacinto, and they marched with the Texas veterans who rejoiced at the birth of Texas independence. It is the spirit of the Alamo that moved above the Texas soldiers as they charged like demigods through a thousand battlefields, and it is the spirit of the Alamo that whispers from their graves held in every State of the Union, ennobling their dust, their soil, that was crimsoned with their blood.

In the spirit of this inspiration and in the thrill of the amazing growth that surrounds you, my young friends, it will be strange if the young men of Texas do not carry the lone star into the heart of the struggle. The South needs her sons to-day more than when she summoned them to the forum to maintain her political supremacy, more than when the bugle called them to the field to defend issues put to the arbitrament of the sword. Her old body is instinct with appeal calling on us to come and give her fuller independence than she has ever sought in field or forum. It is ours to show that as she prospered with

cer of the Texan War of Independence. He was one of the three hundred and fifty-seven men massacred at Goliad, by order of Santa Anna, March 27, 1836.

Lone Star: The emblem of Texas.

slaves she shall prosper still more with freemen;
ours to see that from the lists she entered in poverty she shall emerge in prosperity; ours to carry
the transcending traditions of the old South from
which none of us can in honor or in reverence
depart, unstained and unbroken into the new.

Shall we fail? Shall the blood of the old South
— the best strain that ever uplifted human en-
deavor — that ran like water at duty's call and
never stained where it touched — shall this blood
that pours into our veins through a century lu-
minous with achievement, for the first time falter
and be driven back from irresolute heart, when
the old South, that left us a better heritage in
manliness and courage than in broad and rich
acres, calls us to settle problems?

A soldier lay wounded on a hard-fought field,
the roar of the battle had died away, and he rested
in the deadly stillness of its aftermath. Not a
sound was heard as he lay there, sorely smitten
and speechless, but the shriek of wounded and the
sigh of the dying soul, as it escaped from the
tumult of earth into the unspeakable peace of the
stars. Off over the field flickered the lanterns of
the surgeons with the litter bearers, searching that
they might take away those whose lives could be
saved and leave in sorrow those who were doomed

Aftermath: A second crop of grass mown in the
same season.

to die with pleading eyes through the darkness. This poor soldier watched, unable to turn or speak as the lantern drew near. At last the light flashed in his face, and the surgeon, with kindly face, bent over him, hesitated a moment, shook his head, and was gone, leaving the poor fellow alone with death. He watched in patient agony as they went from one part of the field to another.

As they came back the surgeon bent over him again. " I believe if this poor fellow lives to sundown to-morrow he will get well." And again leaving him, not to death but with hope; all night long these words fell into his heart as the dew fell from the stars upon his lips, "if he but lives till sundown, he will get well."

He turned his weary head to the east and watched for the coming sun. At last the stars went out, the east trembled with radiance, and the sun, slowly lifting above the horizon, tinged his pallid face with flame. He watched it inch by inch as it climbed slowly up the heavens. He thought of life, its hopes and ambitions, its sweetness and its raptures, and he fortified his soul against despair until the sun had reached high noon. It sloped down its slow descent, and his life was ebbing away and his heart was faltering, and he needed stronger stimulants to make him stand the struggle until the end of the day had come. He thought of his far-off home, the blessed house resting in tranquil peace with the roses climbing to its door, and the trees whispering to its windows and dozing in the sunshine, the orchard and the little brook running like a silver thread through the forest.

" If I live till sundown I will see it again. I will walk down the shady lane; I will open the battered gate, and the mocking-bird shall call to me from the orchard, and I will drink again at the old mossy spring."

And he thought of the wife who had come from the neighboring farmhouse and put her hands shyly in his, and brought sweetness to his life and light to his home.

" If I live till sundown I shall look once more into her deep and loving eyes and press her brown head once more to my aching breast."

And he thought of the old father, patient in prayer, bending lower and lower every day under his load of sorrow and old age.

" If I but live till sundown I shall see him again and wind my strong arm about his feeble body, and his hands shall rest upon my head while the unspeakable healing of his blessing falls into my heart."

And he thought of the little children that clambered on his knees and tangled their little hands into his heartstrings, making to him such music as the world shall not equal or heaven surpass.

" If I live till sundown they shall again find

my parched lips with their warm mouths, and
their little fingers shall run once more over my
face."

And he then thought of his old mother, who
gathered these children about her and breathed
her old heart afresh in their brightness and at-
tuned her old lips anew to their prattle, that she
might live till her big boy came home.

"If I live till sundown I will see her again,
and I will rest my head at my old place on her
knees, and weep away all memory of this deso-
late night." And the Son of God, who died for
men, bending from the stars, put the hand that
had been nailed to the cross on the ebbing life
and held on the staunch until the sun went down
and the stars came out and shone down in the
brave man's heart and blurred in his glistening
eyes, and the lanterns of the surgeons came and
he was taken from death to life.

The world is a battle-field strewn with the
wrecks of government and institutions, of theories
and of faiths that have gone down in the ravage
of years. On this field lies the South, sown with
her problems. Upon this field swings the lanterns of God. Amid the carnage walks the Great
Physician. Over the.South he bends. "If ye
but live until to-morrow's sundown ye shall endure, my countrymen." Let us for her sake turn
our faces to the east and watch as the soldier
watched for the coming sun. Let us staunch her

wounds and hold steadfast. The sun mounts the skies. As it descends to us, minister to her and stand constant at her side for the sake of our children and of generations unborn that shall suffer if she fails. And when the sun has gone down and the day of her probation has ended and the stars have rallied her heart, the lanterns shall be swung over the field and the Great Physician shall lead her up from trouble into content, from suffering into peace, from death to life.

Let every man here pledge himself in this high and ardent hour, as I pledge myself and the boy that shall follow me; every man himself and his son, hand to hand and heart to heart, that in death and earnest loyalty, in patient painstaking and care, he shall watch her interest, advance her fortune, defend her fame and guard her honor as long as life shall last. Every man in the sound of my voice, under the deeper consecration he offers to the Union, will consecrate himself to the South. Have no ambition but to be first at her feet and last at her service,— no hope but, after a long life of devotion, to sink to sleep in her bosom, as a little child sleeps at his mother's breast and rests untroubled in the light of her smile.

With such consecrated service, what could we not accomplish; what riches we should gather for her; what glory and prosperity we should render to the Union; what blessings we should gather unto the universal harvest of humanity. As I think of it, a vision of surpassing beauty unfolds to my eyes. I see a South, a home of fifty millions of people, who rise up every day to call her blessed; her cities, vast hives of industry and of thrift; her country-sides the treasures from which their resources are drawn; her streams vocal with whirring spindles; her valleys tranquil in the white and gold of the harvest; her mountains showering down the music of bells, as her slow-moving flocks and herds go forth from their folds; her rulers honest and her people loving, and her homes happy and their hearthstones bright, and their waters still, and their pastures green, and her conscience clear; her wealth diffused and poor-houses empty, her churches earnest and all creeds lost in the gospel. Peace and sobriety walking hand in hand through her borders; honor in her homes; uprightness in her midst; plenty in her fields; straight and simple faith in the hearts of her sons and daughters; her two races walking together in peace and contentment; sunshine everywhere and all the time, and night falling on her gently as from the wings of the unseen dove.

All this, my country, and more can we do for you. As I look the vision grows, the splendor deepens, the horizon falls back, the skies open their everlasting gates, and the glory of the Almighty God streams through as He looks down on His people who have given themselves unto Him, and leads them from one triumph to another until they have reached a glory unspeakable, and the whirling stars, as in their courses through Arcturus they run to the milky way, shall not look down on a better people or happier land.

Arcturus: A fixed star of the first magnitude.

At the Boston Banquet

In his speech at the annual banquet of the Boston Merchants' Association in December, 1889, Mr. Grady said:

MR. PRESIDENT: Bidden by your invitation to a discussion of the race problem — forbidden by occasion to make a political speech — I appreciate in trying to reconcile orders with propriety the predicament of the little maid, who, bidden to learn to swim, was yet adjured, " Now, go, my darling, hang your clothes on a hickory limb, and don't go near the water."

The stoutest apostle of the church, they say, is the missionary, and the missionary, wherever he unfurls his flag, will never find himself in deeper need of unction and address than I, bidden to-night to plant the standard of a Southern Democrat in Boston's banquet-hall, and discuss the problem of the races in the home of Phillips and of Sumner. But, Mr. President, if a purpose

Wendell Phillips (1811-1884) of Massachusetts: A scholar and orator, distinguished for his hostility to the institution of slavery. He was for some years president of the Anti-Slavery Society.

Charles Sumner (1811-1874) of Massachusetts: A lawyer and statesman, one of the most earnest opponents of slavery.

92

to speak in perfect frankness and sincerity; if
earnest understanding of the vast interests involved; if a consecrating sense of what disaster
may follow further misunderstanding and estrangement, if these may be counted to steady
undisciplined speech and to strengthen an untried
arm — then, sir, I find the courage to proceed.

Happy am I that this mission has brought my
feet at last to press New England's historic soil,
and my eyes to the knowledge of her beauty and
her thrift. Here, within touch of Plymouth Rock
and Bunker Hill — where Webster thundered
and Longfellow sang, Emerson thought and
Channing preached — here in the cradle of American letters, and almost of American liberty, I
hasten to make the obeisance that every American
owes New England when first he stands uncovered in her mighty presence. Strange appari-
tion! This stern and unique figure — carved
from the ocean and the wilderness — its majesty
kindling and growing amid the storms of winters
and of wars — until at last the gloom was broken,
its beauty disclosed in the sunshine, and the heroic
workers rested at its base — while startled kings
and emperors gazed and marveled that from the
rude touch of this handful, cast on a bleak and
unknown shore, should have come the embodied

William Ellery Channing (1780-1842) of Rhode
Island: A distinguished Unitarian clergyman and
an eloquent writer.

genius of human government and the perfected model of human liberty! God bless the memory of those immortal workers and prosper the fortunes of their living sons and perpetuate the inspirations of their handiwork.

Two years ago, sir, I spoke some words in New York that caught the attention of the North. As I stand here to reiterate, as I have done everywhere, every word I then uttered — to declare that the sentiments I then avowed were universally approved in the South — I realize that the confidence begotten by that speech is largely responsible for my presence here to-night. I should dishonor myself if I betrayed that confidence by uttering one insincere word or by withholding one essential element of the truth. Apropos of this last, let me confess, Mr. President — before the praise of New England has died on my lips — that I believe the best product of her present life is the procession of 17,000 Vermont Democrats that for twenty-two years, undiminished by death, unrecruited by birth or conversion, have marched over their rugged hills, cast their Democratic ballots, and gone back home to pray for their unregenerate neighbors, and awake to read the record of 25,000 Republican majority. May God of the helpless and the heroic help them — and may their sturdy tribe increase!

Far to the south, Mr. President, separated from this section by a line, once defined in irrepressible difference, once traced in fraticidal blood, and now, thank God, but a vanishing shadow, lies the fairest and richest domain of this earth. It is the home of a brave and hospitable people. There, is centered all that can please or prosper humankind. A perfect climate above a fertile soil, yields to the husbandman every product of the temperate zone. There, by night the cotton whitens beneath the stars, and by day the wheat locks the sunshine in its bearded sheaf. In the same field the clover steals the fragrance of the wind, and the tobacco catches the quick aroma of the rains. There, are mountains stored with exhaustless treasures; forests, vast and primeval, and rivers that, tumbling or loitering, run wanton to the sea. Of the three essential items of all industries — cotton, iron, and wool — that region has easy control. In cotton, a fixed monopoly — in iron, proven supremacy — in timber, the reserve supply of the Republic. From this assured and permanent advantage, against which artificial conditions cannot much longer prevail, has grown an amazing system of industries. Not maintained by human contrivance of tariff or capital, afar off from the fullest and cheapest source of supply, but resting in Divine assurance, within touch of field and mine and forest — not set amid costly farms from which

Fratricidal: From, or relating to, fratricide, the murder of a brother.

competition has driven the farmer in despair, but amid cheap and sunny lands, rich with agriculture, to which neither season nor soil has set a limit — this system of industries is mounting to a splendor that shall dazzle and illumine the world.

That, sir, is the picture and the promise of my home — a land better and fairer than I have told you, and yet but fit setting, in its material excellence, for the loyal and gentle quality of its citizenship. Against that, sir, we have New England, recruiting the Republic from its sturdy loins, shaking from its overcrowded hives new swarms of workers and touching this land all over with its energy and its courage. And yet, while in the El Dorado of which I have told you, but fifteen per cent. of lands are cultivated, its mines scarcely touched and its population so scant that, were it set equi-distant, the sound of the human voice could not be heard from Virginia to Texas — while on the threshold of nearly every house in New England stands a son, seeking with troubled eyes some new land to which to carry his modest patrimony, the strange fact remains that in 1880 the South had fewer Northern-born

El Dorado: A fabulous region of South America, surpassing all others in its riches, especially of gold and gems; hence, as here, any country, real or imaginary, abounding in gold or other precious products of nature.

citizens than she had in 1870 — fewer in '70 than
in '60. Why is this? Why is it, sir, though the
sectional line be now but a mist that the breath
may dispel, fewer men of the North have crossed
it over to the South than when it was crimson
with the best blood of the Republic, or even
when the slaveholder stood guard every inch of
its way?

There can be but one answer. It is the very
problem we are now to consider. The key that
opens that problem will unlock to the world the
fairer half of this Republic, and free the halted
feet of thousands whose eyes are already kindled
with its beauty. Better than this, it will open
the hearts of brothers for thirty years estranged,
and clasp in lasting comradeship a million hands
now withheld in doubt. Nothing, sir, but this
problem, and the suspicions it breeds, hinders
a clear understanding and a perfect union. Nothing else stands between us and such love as bound
Georgia and Massachusetts at Valley Forge and
Yorktown, chastened by the sacrifices at Manassas and Gettysburg, and illumined with the coming of better work and a nobler destiny than was
ever wrought with the sword or sought at the
cannon's mouth.

If this does not invite your patient hearing
to-night — hear one thing more. My people,
your brothers in the South — brothers in blood,
in destiny, in all that is best in our past and future

— are so beset with this problem that their very existence depends upon its right solution. Nor are they wholly to blame for its presence. The slave-ships of the Republic sailed from your ports — the slaves worked in our fields. You will not defend the traffic, nor I the institution. But I do hereby declare that in its wise and humane administration, in lifting the slave to heights of which he had not dreamed in his savage home, and giving him a happiness he has not yet found in freedom — our fathers left their sons a saving and excellent heritage. In the storm of war this institution was lost. I thank God as heartily as you do that human slavery is gone forever from the American soil.

But the freedman remains. With him a problem without precedent or parallel. Note its appalling conditions. Two utterly dissimilar races on the same soil — with equal political and civil rights — almost equal in numbers, but terribly unequal in intelligence and responsibility — each pledged against fusion — one for a century in servitude to the other, and freed at last by a desolating war — the experiment sought by neither, but approached by both with

Slave-ships of the Republic: The first slaves were brought by a Dutch ship to Virginia in 1619. Thereafter ships of Old England, and New England engaged in the slave trade and brought negroes to Virginia and the other colonies north and south.

doubt — these are the conditions. Under these, adverse at every point, we are required to carry these two races in peace and honor to the end. Never, sir, has such a task been given to mortal stewardship. Never before in this Republic has the white race divided on the rights of an alien race. The red man was cut down as a weed, because he hindered the way of the American citizen. The yellow man was shut out of this Republic because he is an alien and inferior. The red man was owner of the land — the yellow man highly civilized and assimilable — but they hindered both sections and are gone!

But the black man, affecting but one section, is clothed with every privilege of government and pinned to the soil, and my people commanded to make good at any hazard and at any cost, his full and equal heirship of American privilege and prosperity. It matters not that wherever the whites and blacks have touched, in any era or any clime, there has been irreconcilable violence. It matters not that no two races, however similar, have lived anywhere at any time on the same soil with equal rights in peace. In spite of these things we are commanded to make good this

Red man was cut down, &c.: Trace the history of the Indian from the sixteenth century to the twentieth.

Yellow man: The Chinese, shut out of the United States by immigration laws.

change of American policy which has not perhaps changed American prejudice — to make
certain here what has elsewhere been impossible
between whites and blacks — and to reverse, under the very worst conditions, the universal verdict of racial history. And driven, sir, to this
superhuman task with an impatience that brooks
no delay, a rigor that accepts no excuse, and a
suspicion that discourages frankness and sincerity. We do not shrink from this trial. It is so
interwoven with our industrial fabric that we
cannot disentangle it if we would — so bound up
in our honorable obligation to the world, that we
would not if we could. Can we solve it? The
God who gave it into our hands, He alone can
know. But this the weakest and wisest of us do
know ; we can not solve it with less than your tol-
erant and patient sympathy — with less than the
knowledge that the blood that runs in your veins
is our blood — and that when we have done our
best, whether the issue be lost or won, we shall
feel your strong arms about us and hear the beat-
ing of your approving hearts.

The resolute, clear-headed, broad-minded men
of the South — the men whose genius made glorious every page of the first seventy years of

Men whose genius made glorious, &c.: Such men
as George Washington, Patrick Henry, Richard
Henry Lee, Thomas Jefferson, John Randolph, John
Marshall, William Wirt, Charles Pinckney, James

American history — whose courage and fortitude you tested in five years of the fiercest war — whose energy has made bricks without straw and spread splendor amid the ashes of their war-wasted homes — these men wear this problem in their hearts and their brains, by day and by night. They realize, as you cannot, what this problem means — what they owe to this kindly and dependent race — the measure of their debt to the world in whose despite they defended and maintained slavery. And though their feet are hindered in its undergrowth and their march encumbered with its burdens, they have lost neither the patience from which comes clearness nor the faith from which comes courage. Nor, sir, when in passionate moments is disclosed to them that vague and awful shadow, with its lurid abysses and its crimson stains, into which I pray God they may never go, are they struck with more of apprehension than is needed to complete their consecration!

Such is the temper of my people. But what of the problem itself? Mr. President, we need not go one step further unless you concede right here the people I speak for are as honest, as sensible, and as just as your people, seeking as

Madison, James Monroe, Henry Clay, John Calhoun, Andrew Jackson, William Henry Harrison, John Tyler, James K. Polk, Zachary Taylor, Matthew Fontaine Maury.

earnestly as you would in their place, rightly to
solve the problem that touches them at every
vital point. If you insist that they are ruffians,
blindly striving with bludgeon and shotgun to
plunder and oppress a race, then I shall sacrifice my self-respect and tax your patience in vain.
But admit that they are men of common sense and
common honesty — wisely modifying an environ-
ment they cannot wholly disregard — guiding and
controlling as best they can the vicious and ir-
responsible of either race — compensating error
with frankness and retrieving in patience what
they lose in passion — and conscious all the time
that wrong means ruin,— admit this, and we may
reach an understanding to-night.

The President of the United States in his late
message to Congress, discussing the plea that
the South should be left to solve this problem,
asks: " Are they at work upon it? What solution do they offer? When will the black man
cast a free ballot? When will he have the civil
rights that are his?" I shall not here protest
against the partisanry that, for the first time in
our history in time of peace, has stamped with the
great seal of our government a stigma upon the
people of a great and loyal section, though I
gratefully remember that the great dead soldier,

Stigma: A brand, or mark, made with a burning
iron; hence, as here, mark of shame, a reproach
on one's reputation.

who held the helm of state for the eight stormy years of reconstruction, never found need for such a step; and though there is no personal sacrifice I would not make to remove this cruel and unjust imputation on my people from the archives of my country!

But, sir, backed by a record on every page of which is progress, I venture to make earnest and respectful answer to the questions that are asked. I bespeak your patience, while with vigorous plainness of speech, seeking your judgment rather than your applause, I proceed step by step. We give to the world this year a crop of 7,500,000 bales of cotton, worth $45,-000,000, and its cash equivalent in grain, grasses, and fruit. This enormous crop could not have come from the hands of sullen and discontented labor. It comes from peaceful fields, in which laughter and gossip rise above the hum of industry and contentment runs with the singing plow.

It is claimed that this ignorant labor is defrauded of its just hire. I present the tax-books of Georgia, which show that the negro, 25 years

Archives: Places in which public records are kept; hence, as here, public records and papers.

We give to the world this year, &c.: The cotton crop for the season of 1902-1903 is 10,727,559 bales, valued at $480,770,282.

I present the tax-books of Georgia, &c.: During the seven years from 1895 to 1902 the negroes in

ago a slave, has in Georgia alone $10,000,000 of assessed property, worth twice that much. Does not that record honor him and vindicate his neighbors? What people. penniless, illiterate, has done so well? For every Afro-American agitator, stirring the strife in which alone he prospers, I can show you a thousand negroes, happy in their cabin homes, tilling their own land by day, and at night taking from the lips of their children the helpful message their State sends them from the schoolhouse door. And the schoolhouse itself bears testimony. In Georgia we added last year $250,000 to the school fund, making a total of more than $1,000,000 — and this in the face of prejudice not yet conquered — of the fact that the whites are assessed for $368,000,000, the blacks for $10,000,000, and yet 49 per cent. of the beneficiaries are black children — and in the doubt of many wise men if education helps, or can help, our problem. Charleston, with her taxable values cut half in two since 1860, pays

Georgia increased their holdings in land to 1,175,291 acres — a gain of 136,467 acres. At the end of the seven years they owned city and town property to the amount of $4,389,422 — a gain of $47,356. They owned household and kitchen furniture to the sum of $1,688,541 — a gain of $365,847. They owned horses, mules, etc., to the amount of $2,985,831 — a gain of $696,981. At the end of the seven years their aggregate property amounted to $15,188,069 — a gain of $2,247,239.— Hon. Martin V. Calvin of Georgia.

more in proportion for public schools than Boston. Although it is easier to give much out of much than little out of little, the South with one-seventh of the taxable property of the country, with relatively larger debt, having received only one-twelfth as much public land, and having back of its tax-books none of the half billion of bonds that enrich the North — and though it pays annually $26,000,000 to your section as pensions — yet gives nearly one-sixth of the public school fund. The South since 1865 has spent $122,-000,000 in education, and this year is pledged to $37,000,000 for State and city schools, although the blacks, paying one-thirtieth of the taxes, get nearly one-half of the fund.

Go into our fields and see whites and blacks working side by side, on our buildings in the same squad, in our shops at the same forge. Often the blacks crowd the whites from work, or lower wages by greater need or simpler habits, and yet are permitted because we want to bar them from no avenue in which their feet are fitted to tread. They could not there be elected orators of the white universities, as they have been here, but they do enter there a hundred useful trades that are closed against them here. We hold it better and wiser to tend the weeds in the garden than to water the exotic in the window. In the South, there are negro lawyers, teachers, editors, dentists, doctors, preachers, multiplying with the increasing ability of their race to support them. In villages and towns they have their military companies equipped from the armories of the State, their churches and societies built and supported largely by their neighbors. What is the testimony of the courts? In penal legislation we have steadily reduced felonies to misdemeanors, and have led the world in mitigating punishment for crime, that we might save, as far as possible, this dependent race from its own weakness. In our penitentiary record 60 per cent. of the prosecutors are negroes, and in every court the negro criminal strikes the colored juror, that white men may judge his case. In the North, one negro in every 466 is in jail — in the South only one in 1,865. In the North the percentage of negro prisoners is six times as great as native whites — in the South, only four times as great. If prejudice wrongs him in Southern courts, the record shows it to be deeper in Northern courts.

I assert here, and a bar as intelligent and upright as the bar of Massachusetts will solemnly indorse my assertion, that in the Southern courts, from highest to lowest, pleading for life, liberty, or property, the negro has distinct advantage

Felonies: In American law, offences of a high grade punishable by death or by a term of imprisonment.

Misdemeanors: Crimes less than felonies, of less consequence and lighter punishment.

because he is a negro, apt to be overreached, op-
pressed — and that this advantage reaches from
the juror in making his verdict to the judge in
measuring his sentence. Now, Mr. President,
can it be seriously maintained that we are terror-
izing the people from whose willing hands come
every year $1,000,000,000 of farm crops? Or
have robbed a people, who twenty-five years from
unrewarded slavery have amassed in one State
$20,000,000 of property? Or that we intend to
oppress the people we are arming every day? Or
deceive them when we are educating them to the
utmost limit of our ability? Or outlaw them
when we work side by side with them? Or re-
enslave them under legal forms when for their
benefit we have even imprudently narrowed the
limit of felonies and mitigated the severity of
law? My fellow countryman, as you yourself
may sometimes have to appeal to the bar of human judgment for justice and for right, give to
my people to-night the fair and unanswerable
conclusion of these incontestible facts.

But it is claimed that under this fair seeming
there is disorder and violence. This I admit.
And there will be until there is one ideal community on earth after which we may pattern.
But how widely it is misjudged! It is hard to
measure with exactness whatever touches the
negro. His helplessness, his isolation, his century of servitude, these dispose us to emphasize

and magnify his wrongs. This disposition, inflamed by prejudice and partisanry, has led to injustice and delusion. Lawless men may ravage
a county in Iowa and it is accepted as an incident — in the South a drunken row is declared
to be the fixed habit of the community. Regulators may whip vagabonds in Indiana by platoons,
and it scarcely arrests attention — a chance col-
lision in the South among relatively the same
classes is gravely accepted as evidence that one
race is destroying the other. We might as well
claim that the Union was ungrateful to the colored soldiers who followed its flag, because a
Grand Army post in Connecticut closed its doors
to a negro veteran, as for you to give racial significance to every incident in the South or to
accept exceptional grounds as the rule of our society. I am not one of those who becloud American honor with the parade of the outrages of
either section, and belie American character by
declaring them to be significant and representative. I prefer to maintain that they are neither,
and stand for nothing but the passion and the
sin of our poor fallen humanity. If society,

Regulators: Those who regulate; in the United
States, men who, when ordinary legal authority fails
or is wanting, band themselves together to punish
crime and regulate society.
Platoons: Groups of men; in military term, a
division of a company.

like a machine, were no stronger than its weakest part, I should despair of both sections. But, knowing that society, sentient and responsible in every fibre, can mend and repair until the whole has the strength of the best, I despair of neither.

These gentlemen who come with me here, knit into Georgia's busy life as they are, never saw, I dare assert, an outrage committed on a negro! And if they did, not one of you would be swifter to prevent or punish. It is through them, and the men who think with them — making nine-tenths of every Southern community — that these two races have been carried thus far with less of violence than would have been possible anywhere else on earth. And in their fairness and courage and steadfastness — more than in all the laws that can be passed or all the bayonets that can be mustered — is the hope of our future.

When will the black cast a free ballot? When ignorance anywhere is not dominated by the will of the intelligent; when the laborer anywhere casts a vote unhindered by his boss; when the vote of the poor anywhere is not influenced by the power of the rich; when the strong and the steadfast do not everywhere control the suffrage of the weak and shiftless — then and not till then will the ballot of the negro be free. The white people of the South are banded, Mr. President, not in prejudice against the blacks — not in sectional estrangement, not in the hope of political dominion — but in a deep and abiding necessity. Here is this vast ignorant and purchasable vote —clannish, credulous, impulsive and passionate— tempting every art of the demagogue, but insensible to the appeal of the statesman. Wrongly started, in that it was led into alienation from its neighbor and taught to rely on the protection of an outside force, it cannot be merged and lost in the two great parties through logical currents, for it lacks political conviction and even that information on which conviction must be based. It must remain a faction — strong enough in every community to control on the slightest division of the whites. Under that division it becomes the prey of the cunning and unscrupulous of both parties. Its credulity is imposed on, its patience inflamed, its cupidity tempted, its impulses misdirected — and even its superstition made to play its part in a campaign in which every interest of society is jeopardized and every approach to the ballot-box debauched. It is against such campaigns as this — the folly and the bitterness and the danger of which every Southern community has drunk deeply — that the white people of the South are banded together. Just as you in Massachusetts would be banded if 300,-000 black men — not one in a hundred able to read his ballot — banded in a race instinct, holding against you the memory of a century of slavery, taught by your late conquerors to distrust and oppose you, had already travestied legislation from your statehouse, and in every species of folly or villainy had wasted your substance and exhausted your credit.

But admitting the right of the whites to unite against this tremendous menace, we are challenged with the smallness of our vote. This has long been flippantly charged to be evidence, and has now been solemnly and officially declared to be proof of political turpitude and baseness on our part. Let us see. Virginia — a State now under fierce assault for this alleged crime — cast in 1888 75 per cent. of her vote. Massachusetts,

Turpitude: Baseness; shameful wickedness.

Virginia — a state now under fierce assault, &c.: Nearly one-third of all the males of voting age in the United States do not appear in the last presidential election returns. The total vote in 1900 was 13,959,653, while the total males of voting age was 20,829,819. From which it figures that 6,870,166 of the latter were either disfranchised or indifferent to and neglected their electoral duty. And if you will deduct from that last sum the entire number of negroes of voting age in the forty-five states, being 2,026,851, you get 4,843,315 white males of voting age who were effaced by law and by their own act from the returns, or nearly two and a half times the total number of possible negro voters in the entire Union.

The six states, Maine, Massachusetts, Connecticut, New York, Pennsylvania, and Ohio showed up short of 2,079,632 votes, or 52,781 more than all the negro votes in the United States, North and South.

the State in which I speak, 60 per cent. of her
vote. Was it suppression in Virginia and natural
causes in Massachusetts? Last month Virginia
cast 69 per cent. of her vote, and Massachusetts,
fighting in every district, cast only 49 per cent.
of hers. If Virginia is condemned because 31
per cent. of her vote was silent, how shall this
State escape in which 51 per cent. was dumb?
Let us enlarge this comparison. The sixteen
Southern States in 1888 cast 67 per cent. of their
total vote — the six New England States but 63
per cent. of theirs. By what fair rule shall the
stigma be put upon one section, while the other
escapes? A congressional election in New York
last week, with the polling-place within touch of
every voter, brought out only 6,000 votes of 28,-
000 — and the lack of opposition is assigned as
the natural cause. In a district in my State, in
which an opposition speech has not been heard
in ten years, and the polling-places are miles apart
— under the unfair reasoning of which my section has been a constant victim — the small vote
is charged to be proof of forcible suppression.
In Virginia an average majority of 10,000, under
hopeless division of the minority, was raised to
42,000; in Iowa, in the same election, a majority
of 32,000 was wiped out, and an opposition majority of 8,000 was established. The change of
42,000 votes in Iowa is accepted as political revolution — in Virginia an increase of 30,000 on a

safe majority is declared to be proof of political fraud. I charge these facts and figures home, sir, to the heart and conscience of the American people, who will not assuredly see one section condemned for what another section is excused!

If I can drive them through the prejudice of the partisan, and have .them read and pondered at the fireside of the citizen, I will rest on the judgment there formed and the verdict there rendered!

It is deplorable, sir, that in both sections a larger percentage of the vote is not regularly cast, but more inexplicable that this should be so in New England than in the South. What invites the negro to the ballot-box? He knows that, of all men, it has promised him most and yielded him least. His first appeal to suffrage was the promise of " forty acres and a mule." His second, the threat that Democratic success meant his re-enslavement. Both have proved false in his experience. He looked for a home, and he got the freedman's bank. He fought under the promise of the loaf, and in victory was

Inexplicable: Not explainable; not capable of being explained or accounted for.

" Forty acres and a mule ": At the close of the war between the states demagogues led negroes into the Republican party by telling them that Lincoln had said that the negroes should each have " forty acres and a mule," and that they were to receive these on the triumph of the Republican party.

denied the crumbs. Discouraged and deceived, he has realized at last that his best friends are his neighbors, with whom his lot is cast, and whose prosperity is bound up in his — and that he has gained nothing in politics to compensate the loss of their confidence and sympathy that is at last his best and his enduring hope. And so, without leaders or organization — and lacking the resolute heroism of my party friends in Vermont that makes their hopeless march over the hills a high and inspiring pilgrimage — he shrewdly measures the occasional agitator, balances his little account with politics, touches up his mule and jogs down the furrow, letting the mad world jog as it will!

The negro vote can never control in the South, and it would be well if partisans in the North would understand this. I have seen the white people of a State set about by black hosts until their fate seemed sealed. But, sir, some brave man, banding them together, would rise, as Elisha rose in beleaguered Samaria, and touching their eyes with faith, bid them look abroad to see the very air " filled with the chariots of Israel and the horsemen thereof." If there is any human force that cannot be withstood, it is the power of the banded intelligence and responsibility of a free community. Against it, numbers

As Elisha rose, &c.: 2 Kings ii., 9-12.

and corruption cannot prevail. It cannot be forbidden in the law or divorced in force. It is the inalienable right of every free community — and the just and righteous safeguard against an ignorant or corrupt suffrage. It is on this, sir, that we rely in the South. Not the cowardly menace of mask or shotgun; but the peaceful majesty of intelligence and responsibility, massed and unified for the protection of its homes and the preservation of its liberty. That, sir, is our reliance and our hope, and against it all the powers of the earth shall not prevail.

It was just as certain that Virginia would come back to the unchallenged control of her white race — that before the moral and material power of her people once more unified, opposition would crumble until its last desperate leader was left alone vainly striving to rally his disordered hosts — as that night should fade in the kindling glory of the sun. You may pass force bills, but they will not avail. You may surrender your own liberties to Federal election law, you may submit, in fear of a necessity that does not exist, that the very form of this government may be changed — this old State that holds in its charter the boast that " it

Force bills: A law by which the Federal government temporarily took control of matters ordinarily handled by State governments was so called during the reconstruction period.

is a free and independent commonwealth "— it
may deliver its election machinery into the hands
of the government it helped to create — but
never, sir, will a single State of this Union, North
or South, be delivered again to the control of
an ignorant and inferior race. We wrested our
State government from negro supremacy when
the Federal drumbeat rolled closer to the ballot-
box and Federal bayonets hedged it deeper about
than will ever again be permitted in this free
government. But, sir, though the cannon of this
Republic thundered in every voting district of
the South, we still should find in the mercy of
God the means and the courage to prevent its re-
establishment!

I regret, sir, that my section, hindered with
this problem, stands in seeming estrangement to
the North. If, sir, any man will point out to
me a path down which the white people of the
South divided may walk in peace and honor, I
will take that path though I take it alone — for
at the end, and nowhere else, I fear, is to be
found the full prosperity of my section and the
full restoration of this Union. But, sir, if the
negro had not been enfranchised, the South would
have been divided and the Republic united. What
solution, then, can we offer for this problem?
Time alone can disclose it to us. We simply report progress and ask your patience. If the problem be solved at all — and I firmly believe it will,

though nowhere else has it been — it will be solved by the people most deeply bound in interest, most deeply pledged in honor to its solution. I had rather see my people render back this question rightly solved than to see them gather all the spoils over which faction has contended since Catiline conspired and Cæsar fought.

Meantime we treat the negro fairly, measuring to him justice in the fullness the strong should give to the weak, and leading him in the steadfast ways of citizenship that he may no longer be the prey of the unscrupulous and the sport of the thoughtless. We open to him every pursuit in which he can prosper, and seek to broaden his training and capacity. We seek to hold his confidence and friendship, and to pin him to the soil with ownership, that he may catch in the fire of his own hearthstone that sense of responsibility the shiftless can never know. And we gather him into that alliance of intelligence and responsibility that, though it now runs close to racial lines, welcomes the responsible and intelligent of any race. By this course, confirmed in our judgment and justified in the progress already made, we hope to progress slowly but surely to the end.

The love we feel for that race you cannot measure nor comprehend. As I attest it here, the

Catiline conspired, &c.: See note on page 62.

spirit of my old black mammy from her home up
there looks down to bless, and through the tumult
of this night steals the sweet music of her croon-
ings as thirty years ago she held me in her black
arms and led me smiling into sleep. This scene
vanishes as I speak, and I catch a vision of an
old Southern home, with its lofty pillars, and its
white pigeons fluttering down through the golden
air. I see women with strained and anxious
faces and children alert yet helpless. I see night
come down with its dangers and its apprehen-
sions, and in a big homely room I feel on my tired
head the touch of loving hands — now worn and
wrinkled, but fairer to me yet than the hands of
mortal woman, and stronger yet to lead me than
the hands of mortal man — as they lay a mother's
blessing there while at her knees, the truest
altar I yet have found — I thank God that she is
safe in her sanctuary, because her slaves, sen-
tinel in the silent cabin or guard at her chamber
door, put a black man's loyalty between her and
danger.

I catch another vision. The crisis of battle —
a soldier struck, staggering, fallen. I see a slave,
scuffling through the smoke, winding his black
arms about the fallen form, reckless of the hurtling death — bending his trusty face to catch the
words that tremble on the stricken lips, so wrest-

Hurtling: Clashing; meeting with violence. The
word is a diminutive of *hurt*.

ling meantime with agony that he would lay down his life in his master's stead. I see him by the weary bedside, ministering with uncomplaining patience, praying with all his humble heart that God will lift his master up, until death comes in mercy and in honor to still the soldier's agony and seal the soldier's life. I see him by the open grave, mute, motionless, uncovered, suffering for the death of him who in life fought against his freedom. I see him when the mound is heaped and the great drama of his life is closed, turn away and with downcast eyes and uncertain step start out into new and strange fields, faltering, struggling, but moving on, until his shambling figure is lost in the light of this better and brighter day. And from the grave comes a voice saying: "Follow him! Put your arms about him in his need, even as he put his about me. Be his friend as he was mine." And out into this new world — strange to me as to him, dazzling, bewildering both — I follow! And may God forget my people — when they forget these.

Whatever the future may hold for them — whether they plod along in the servitude from which they have never been lifted since the Cyrenian was laid hold upon by the Roman soldiers and made to bear the cross of the fainting Christ — whether they find homes again in Africa, and thus hasten the prophecy of the psalmist who

Cyrenian: See Luke xxiii., 26.

said : " And suddenly Ethiopia shall hold out her hands unto God "— whether, forever dislocated and separated, they remain a weak people beset by stronger, and exist as the Turk, who lives in the jealousy rather than in the conscience of Europe — or whether in this miraculous Republic they break through the caste of twenty centuries and, belying universal history, reach the full stature of citizenship, and in peace maintain it — we shall give them uttermost justice and abiding friendship. And whatever we do, into whatever seeming estrangement we may be driven, nothing shall disturb the love we bear this Republic, or mitigate our consecration to its service.

I stand here, Mr. President, to profess no new loyalty. When General Lee, whose heart was the temple of our hopes and whose arm was clothed with our strength, renewed his allegiance to the government at Appo-

" And suddenly Ethiopia," &c.: See Psalms lxviii., 31.

The Turk who lives, &c.: Turkey is an effete empire, kept from destruction by the powers of Europe from fear lest in its partition the balance of power should be disturbed. It has become known since 1844 as the " Sick man of the East " from the words of Czar Nicholas of Russia: " We have on our hands a sick man, a very sick man. It would be a great misfortune if one of these days he should happen to die before the necessary arrangements are made. . . . The man is certainly dying, and we must not allow such an event to take us by surprise."

mattox, he spoke from a heart too great to be false, and he spoke for every honest man from Maryland to Texas. From that day to this, Hamilcar has nowhere in the South sworn young Hannibal to hatred and vengeance — but everywhere to loyalty and to love. Witness the soldier standing at the base of a Confederate monument above the graves of his comrades, his empty sleeve tossing in the April wind, adjuring the young men about him to serve as honest and loyal citizens the government against which their fathers fought. This message, delivered from that sacred presence, has gone home to the hearts of my fellows! And, sir, I declare here, if physical courage be always equal to human aspiration, that they would die, sir, if need be, to restore this Republic their fathers fought to dissolve!

Such, Mr. President, is this problem as we see it; such is the temper in which we approach it; such the progress made. What do we ask of you? First, patience; out of this alone can come perfect work. Second, confidence; in this alone can you judge fairly. Third, sympathy; in this you can help us best. Fourth, give us your sons as hostages. When you plant your capital in millions,

Hamilcar, &c.: Hamilcar, a famous Carthaginian general, was the father of the great general, Hannibal. Hamilcar lived in the third century before Christ when Rome was extending her power over the world. He fought against Rome in Sicily, Africa, and Spain, and it is said that he caused his young

send your sons that they may help know how true are our hearts and may help swell the Anglo-Saxon current until it can carry without danger this black infusion. Fifth, loyalty to the Republic — for there is sectionalism in loyalty as in estrangement. This hour little needs the loyalty that is loyal to one section and yet holds the other in enduring suspicion and estrangement. Give us the broad and perfect loyalty that loves and trusts Georgia alike with Massachusetts — that knows no South, no North, no East, no West; but endears with equal and patriotic love every foot of our soil, every State of our Union.

A mighty duty, sir, and a mighty inspiration impels every one of us to-night to lose in patriotic consecration whatever estranges, whatever divides. We, sir, are Americans — and we fight for human liberty. The uplifting force of the American idea is under every throne on earth. France, Brazil — these are our victories. To redeem the earth from kingcraft and oppression — this is our mission. And we shall not fail. God has sown in our soil the seed of his millennial harvest, and he will not lay the sickle to the ripen-

son Hannibal to swear on the altar of their gods eternal hostility to Rome — an oath which was sacredly kept.

Millennial harvest: The millennium, the thousand years mentioned in the twentieth chapter of Revelation during which period Satan will be bound and Christ reign on earth.

ing crop until his full and perfect day has come. Our history, sir, has been a constant and expanding miracle from Plymouth Rock and Jamestown all the way — aye, even from the hour when, from the voiceless and trackless ocean, a new world rose to the sight of the inspired sailor.

As we approach the fourth centennial of that stupendous day — when the old world will come to marvel and to learn, amid our gathered treasures — let us resolve to crown the miracles of our past with the spectacle of a Republic compact, united, indissoluble in the bonds of love — loving from the lakes to the Gulf — the wounds of war healed in every heart as on every hill — serene and resplendent at the summit of human achievement and earthly glory — blazing out the path, and making clear the way up which all the nations of the earth must come in God's appointed time !

Before the Bay State Club

During Mr. Grady's visit to Boston, in 1889, he was a guest of the Bay State Club, before which he delivered the following speech:

Mr. President and Gentlemen: I am confident you will not expect a speech from me this afternoon, especially as my voice is in such a condition that I can hardly talk. I am free to say that it is not a lack of ability to talk, because I am a talker by inheritance. My father was an Irishman, my mother was a woman; both talked. I come by it honestly.

I don't know how I could take up any discussion here or any topic apart from the incidents of the past two days. I saw this morning Plymouth Rock. I was pulled up on top of it and was told to make a speech.

It reminded me of an old friend of mine, Judge Dooley, of Georgia, who was a very provoking fellow and was always getting challenged to duels and never fighting them. He always got out of it by being smarter than the other fellow. One day he went out to fight a man with one leg, and he insisted on bringing along a bee gum and sticking one leg into it so he would have no more flesh exposed than his antagonist. On the occasion I am thinking of, however, he went out to fight with a man who had St. Vitus's dance, and the fellow stood before him holding the pistol cocked and primed, his hand shaking. The judge went quietly and got a forked stick and stuck it up in front of him.

"What's that for?" said the man.

"I want you to shoot with a rest, so that if you hit me you will bore only one hole. If you shoot me that way you will fill me full of holes with one shot."

I was reminded of that and forced to tell my friends that I could not think of speaking on top of Plymouth Rock without a rest.

But I said this, and I want to say it here again, for I never knew how true it was till I had heard myself say it and had taken the evidence of my voice, as well as my thoughts — that there is no spot on earth that I had rather have seen than that. I have a boy who is the pride and the promise of my life, and God knows I want him to be a good citizen and a good man, and there is no spot in all this broad Republic nor in all this world where I had rather have him stand to learn the lessons of right citizenship, of individual liberty, of fortitude and heroism and justice, than the spot on which I stood this morning, reverent and uncovered.

Now, I do not intend to make a political speech,

although when Mr. Cleveland expressed some surprise at seeing me here, I said: " Why I am at home now; I was out visiting last night." I was visiting mighty clever folks, but still I was visiting. Now I am at home.

It is the glory and the promise of Democracy, it seems to me, that its success means more than partisanry can mean. I have been told that what I said helped the Democratic party in this State. Well, the chief joy that I feel at that, and that you feel, is that, beyond that and above it, it helped those larger interests of the Republic, and those essential interests of humanity that for seventy years the Democratic party has stood for, being the guarantor and defender.

Now, Mr. Cleveland last night made — I trust this will not get into the papers — one of the best Democratic speeches I ever heard in my life, and yet all around sat Republicans cheering him to the echo. It is just simply because he pitched his speech on a high key, and because he said things that no man, no matter how partisan he was, could gainsay.

Now it seems to me we do not care much for political success in the South — for a simple question of spoils or of patronage. We wanted to see one Democratic administration since General

Guarantor: One who engages to secure another in any right or possession.

Lee surrendered at Appomattox, just to prove
to the people of this world that the South was not
the wrong-headed and impulsive and passionate
section she was represented to be. I heard last
night from Mr. Cleveland, our great leader, as
he sat by me, that he held to be the miracle of
modern history the conservatism and the temper-
ance and the quiet with which the South accepted
his election, and the few office-seekers in comparison that came from that section to besiege and
importune him.

Now it seems to me that the struggle in this
country, the great fight, the roar and din of which
we already hear, is a fight against the consolida-
tion of power, the concentration of capital, the
diminution of local sovereignty and the dwarfing
of the individual citizen. Boston is the home of
the one section of a nationalist party that claims
that the remedy for all our troubles, the way in
which Dives, who sits inside the gate, shall be
controlled, and the poor Lazarus who sits outside
shall be lifted up, is for the government to usurp
the functions of the citizen and take charge of all
his affairs. It is the Democratic doctrine that
the citizen is the master and that the best guaran-
tee of this government is not garnered powers
at the capital, but diffused intelligence and liberty
among the people.

Dives, who sits, &c.: See Luke xvi., 19-31.

My friend, General Collins — who, by the way, captured my whole State and absolutely conjured the ladies — when he came down there talked about this to us, and he gave us a train of thought that we have improved to advantage.

It is the pride, I believe, of the South, with her simple faith and her homogeneous people, that we elevate there the citizen above the party, and the citizen above everything. We teach a man that his best guide at last is his own conscience, that his sovereignty rests beneath his hat, that his own right arm and his own stout heart are his best dependence; that he should rely on his State for nothing that he can do for himself, and on his government for nothing that his State can do for him; but that he should stand upright and self-respecting, dowering his family in the sweat of his brow, loving to his State, loyal to his Republic, earnest in his allegiance wherever it rests, but building at last his altars above his own hearthstone and shrining his own liberty in his own heart. That is a sentiment that I would not have been afraid to avow last night. And yet it is mighty good democratic doctrine, too.

I went to Washington the other day and I stood on the Capitol hill and my heart beat quick as I looked at the towering marble of my coun-

General Collins: General Patrick Collins, a prominent Bostonian Democrat, who has been mayor of that city.

try's Capitol, and a mist gathered in my eyes as I thought of its tremendous significance, of the armies and the treasury, and the judges and the President, and the Congress and the courts, and all that was gathered there; and I felt that the sun in all its course could not look down on a better sight than that majestic home of a Republic that has taught the world its best lessons of liberty. And I felt that if honor and wisdom and justice abided therein, the world would at last owe that great house, in which the ark of the covenant of my country is lodged, its final uplifting and its regeneration.

But a few days afterwards I went to visit a friend in the country, a modest man, with a quiet country home. It was just a simple, unpretentious house, set about with great trees and encircled in meadow and field rich with the promise of harvest; the fragrance of the pink and the hollyhock in the front yard was mingled with the aroma of the orchard and the garden, and the resonant clucking of poultry and the hum of bees. Inside was quiet, cleanliness, thrift, and comfort.

The Ark of the Covenant: A chest of acacia wood overlaid and lined with gold, which was kept in the Holy of Holies in the Jewish Tabernacle. The ark contained the two tables of stone inscribed with the ten commandments, a pot of manna, and Aaron's rod.

Resonant: Fitted to resound; echoing back.

Outside there stood my friend, the master — a simple, independent, upright man, with no mortgage on his roof, no lien on his growing crops — master of his land and master of himself. There was the old father, an aged and trembling man, but happy in the heart and home of his son. And, as he started to enter his home, the hand of the old man went down on the young man's shoulder, laying there the unspeakable blessing of an honored and honorable father, and ennobling it with the knighthood of the fifth commandment. And as we approached the door the mother came, a happy smile lighting up her face, while with the rich music of her heart she bade her husband and her son welcome to their home. Beyond was the housewife, busy with her domestic affairs, the loving helpmate of her husband. Down the lane came the children after the cows, singing sweetly, as like birds they sought the quiet of their rest.

So the night came down on that house, falling gently as the wing of an unseen dove. And the old man, while a startled bird called from the forest and the trees thrilled with the cricket's cry, and the stars were falling from the sky, called the family around him and took the Bible from the table and called them to their knees. The little baby hid in the folds of its mother's dress while he closed the record of that day by calling down

Lien: A legal claim on property for the satisfaction of a debt.

God's blessing on that simple home. While I gazed, the vision of the marble Capitol faded; forgotten were its treasuries and its majesty; and I said: " Surely here in the homes of the people lodge at last the strength and the responsibility of this government, the hope and the promise of this Republic."

My friends, that is the democracy of the South; that is the democratic doctrine we preach; a doctrine, sir, that is writ above our hearthstones. We aim to make our homes, poor as they are, self-respecting and independent. We try to make them temples of refinement, in which our daughters may learn that woman's best charm and strength is her gentleness and her grace, and temples of liberty in which our sons may learn that no power can justify and no treasure repay for the surrender of the slightest right of a free individual American citizen.

Now you do not know how we love you Democrats. Had we better print that? Yes, we do, of course we do. If a man does not love his home folks, whom should he love? We know how gallant a fight you have made here, not as hard and hopeless as our friends in Vermont, but still an up-hill fight. You have been doing better, much better.

Now, gentlemen, I have some mighty good Democrats here. There is one of the fattest and best in the world, sitting right over there (pointing to his partner, Mr. Howell).

You want to know about the South. My friends, we representative men will tell you about it. I just want to say that we have had a hard time down there.

When my partner came out of the war he didn't have any breeches. That is an actual fact. Well, his wife, one of the best women that ever lived, reared in the lap of luxury, took her old woolen dress that she had worn during the war — and it had been a garment of sorrow and consecration and of heroism — and cut it up and made a good pair of breeches. He started with that pair of breeches and with $5 in gold as his capital, and he scraped up boards from amid the ashes of his home, and built him a shanty which love made a home and which courtesy made hospitable. And now I believe he has with him three pairs of breeches and several pairs at home. We have prospered down there.

I attended a funeral once in Pickens county in my State. A funeral is not usually a cheerful object to me unless I could select the subject. I think I could, perhaps, without going a hundred miles from here, find the material for one or two cheerful funerals. Still, this funeral was pecu-

Mr. Howell: Mr. Evan P. Howell, editor of the Atlanta Constitution, which he and Mr. Grady made the foremost paper of the South.

liaily sad. It was a poor "one gallus" fellow, whose breeches struck him under the armpits and hit him at the other end about the knee — he didn't believe in *décolleté* clothes. They buried him in the midst of a marble quarry: they cut through solid marble to make his grave; and yet a little tombstone they put above him was from Vermont. They buried him in the heart of a pine forest, and yet the pine coffin was imported from Cincinnati. They buried him within touch of an iron mine, and yet the nails in his coffin and the iron in the shovel that dug his grave were imported from Pittsburg. They buried him by the side of the best sheep-grazing country on the earth, and yet the wool in the coffin bands and the coffin bands themselves were brought from the North. The South didn't furnish a thing on earth for that funeral but the corpse and the hole in the ground. There they put him away and the clods rattled down on his coffin, and they buried him in a New York coat and a Boston pair of shoes and a pair of breeches from Chicago and a shirt from Cincinnati, leaving him nothing to carry into the next world with him to remind him of the country in which he lived and for which he fought for four years, but the chilled blood in his veins and the marrow in his bones.

Now we have improved on that. We have got

Décolleté: A French word meaning low-necked; a dress which leaves bare neck and shoulders.

the biggest marble-cutting establishment on earth within a hundred yards of the grave. We have got a half-dozen woolen mills right around it, and iron mines, and iron furnaces, and iron factories. We are coming to meet you. We are going to take a noble revenge, as my friend, Mr. Carnegie, said last night, by invading every inch of your territory with iron, as you invaded ours twenty-nine years ago.

[A voice—I want to know if the tariff built up these industries down there?]

Mr. Grady — The tariff? Well, to be perfectly frank with you, I think it helped some; but you can bet your bottom dollar that we are Democrats straight through from the soles of our feet to the top of our heads, and Mr. Cleveland will not have if he runs again, which I am inclined to think he ought to do, a stronger following.

Now, I want to say one word about the reception we had here. It has been a constant revelation of hospitality and kindness and brotherhood from the whole people of this city to myself and my friends. It has touched us beyond measure.

I was struck with one thing last night. Every speaker that arose expressed his confidence in the future and lasting glory of this Republic. There

Mr. Carnegie: Andrew Carnegie was born in Scotland in 1835, and has become distinguished as a steel manufacturer, and by his gifts for public education.

may be men, and there are, who insist on getting
up fratricidal strife, and who infamously fan the
embers of war that they may raise them again into
a blaze. But just as certain as there is a God
in the heavens, when those noisy insects of the
hour have perished in the heat that gave them
life and their pestilent tongues have ceased the
great clock of this Republic will strike the slow-
moving tranquil hours, and the watchman from
the street will cry, " All is well with the Republic;
all is well."

We bring to you, from hearts that yearn for
your confidence and for your love, the message
of fellowship from our homes. This message
comes from consecrated ground. The fields in
which I played were the battlefields of this Republic, hallowed to you with the blood of your soldiers
who died in victory, and doubly sacred to us with
the blood of ours who died undaunted in defeat.
All around my home are set the hills of Kennesaw,
all around the mountains and hills down which
the gray flag fluttered to defeat, and through
which American soldiers from either side charged
like demigods; and I do not think I could bring
you a false message from those old hills and those
sacred fields — witnesses twenty years ago in their
red desolation of the deathless valor of American
arms and the quenchless bravery of American
hearts, and in their white peace and tranquillity
to-day of the imperishable Union of the American

States and the indestructible brotherhood of the American people.

It is likely that I will not again see Bostonians assembled together. I therefore want to take this occasion to thank you, and my excellent friends of last night and those friends who accompanied us this morning, for all that you have done for us since we have been in your city, and to say that whenever any of you come South just speak your name, and remember that Boston or Massachusetts is the watchword, and we will meet you at the gates.

> The monarch may forget the crown
> That on his head so late hath been;
> The bridegroom may forget the bride
> Was made his own but yester e'en;
> The mother may forget the babe
> That smiled so sweetly on her knee;
> But forget thee will I ne'er, Glencairn,
> And all that thou hast done for me.